# pumpkins
# & squashes

**A Reader's Digest Book**
Edited and produced by Mitchell Beazley,
part of Reed International Books Limited

Copyright © Reed International Books Limited 1997
Text copyright © Caroline Boisset 1997
Photography copyright © Reed International Books Limited 1997
Artwork copyright © Reed International Books Limited 1997

Library of Congress Cataloging-in-Publication Data
Boisset, Caroline
Pumpkins & Squashes/Caroline Boisset.
p.  cm.
Includes index.
ISBN 0-89577-957-9
1. Cookery (Pumpkin) 2. Cookery (Squash) 3. Pumpkin. 4. Squashes.
5. Handicraft.  I. Title.
TX803.P93B64  1997
641.6'562—dc21  97-4070

Reader's Digest and Pegasus logo are the trademarks of The Reader's Digest
Association, Inc.

Printed in China

# pumpkins & squashes

caroline boisset

The Reader's Digest Association, Inc.
Pleasantville, New York/Montreal

# contents

# introduction

*The first pumpkin I grew was the brightly colored 'Rouge Vif d'Etampes'. It was one of the few varieties I had ever heard of and the only seed I had been able to buy off the shelf one April when I visited my parents just outside Paris in France. It did well, and by the end of the summer I had three large, beautiful orange pumpkins. I was hooked. I became a pumpkin and squash enthusiast and began searching for ways to use what my garden yielded. The recipes and craft projects in these pages are the result of that search.*

Left  An unusual sight in England,
pumpkins and squashes ripening off in
the sunshine in Sussex, where they have
been grown by Mr. and Mrs. Upton for
over 20 years.

Right  Pumpkins and squashes can
be remarkably decorative, even when
displayed as simply as this.

A year later, my second pumpkin harvest comprised two different varieties, and now, nearly ten years later, I grow some 75 varieties of squashes, pumpkins, and gourds. All are grown from seed, sent from countries across the world, including North America, Australia, New Zealand, South Africa, Italy, France, Germany, as well as from Britain.

It is no accident that pumpkins and squashes, along with many other members of their family, the *Cucurbitae*, fascinate those who have just encountered them and trigger passion in those who start to collect them. They have everything to offer.

Given reasonable growing conditions, most pumpkins and squashes are rewarding to cultivate. The seed is large, easy to sow, and germinates readily. And, with plenty of heat and sun, and some water, it develops quickly — sometimes at an alarming rate — to cover the ground, a fence, or a wall. Summer squashes are ready by midsummer, while winter squashes and pumpkins continue to develop into the most wondrous assortment of shapes and colors into the fall.

This galaxy of forms makes them a versatile medium for the decorator. They can be carved to form lanterns, sculpted or painted, or simply waxed and arranged to display their natural, ornamental qualities. The smaller varieties can be made into table and hanging decorations and the seed into necklaces and collages.

In the kitchen, pumpkins and squashes are immensely versatile. They can be used to make soups and savories; as vegetable dishes and in salads; in breads, cakes, pies, and desserts; and preserved as jams and pickles. It is not only the flesh of the fruit that can be eaten, but also the seed, flowers, shoots, and leaves. Summer squashes are eaten immature and do not keep, but autumn and winter squashes and pumpkins store well, some for several months, making them an important staple in countries where the winters are long and hard.

Above An 18th-century illustration by George Cruikshank with Cinderella looking on as her fairy godmother casts a spell transforming pumpkin (interestingly, not so big), rat, mice, and lizards into a coach, horses, and servants, for the journey to the ball.

Right George Adamson's charming portrayal of a Halloween Roof Party showing the fascination for pumpkin folklore even among glittering New York society.

## History

Pumkins and squashes have a long history, going back many centuries. Pumpkin seeds, estimated to date back to 7,000 B.C., have been found in caves in northeastern Mexico and edible pumpkins and squashes grew in Africa (as far south as Zimbabwe), China, and India as early as the sixth century.

Edible gourds were introduced to Europe and then to Britain around the 16th century, presumably brought back from trips of discovery to the New World. They were certainly well known to the great herbalist John Parkinson, who details the diversity of shapes and colors of both the *pompion* (as pumpkins were then known) and the *long gourd* (presumably a large zucchini) in his famous work *Paradisis in Sole Paradisus Terrestris* (1629). He describes them as "very sweete and pleasant."

A little earlier, in North America, pumpkins were soon adopted by the settlers. It is well documented how in 1623 the Pilgrims served pumpkin pie at their second Thanksgiving. Soup and beer made from pumpkins also became popular among the colonists. European settlers in Virginia were already using squashes as early as 1607.

Pumpkins and squashes were even thought to have medicinal powers. In the 18th century the seeds were used not only as diuretics (in the form of tea) but also for treating tapeworm. It was also believed by some Central Europeans that pumpkin seed built up testosterone by preserving the prostate gland.

But by the second half of the 19th century, the popularity of squash and pumpkin had waned in Britain to such an extent that even culinary guru Mrs. Beeton showed little awareness of their earlier presence when describing the vegetable marrow as a "variety of the gourd family brought from Persia by an East India ship and only recently introduced to Britain."

In North America, Australia, and South Africa, however, the pumpkin remained popular for medicinal use, as well as cookery and crafts. And, to my delight, there has been a resurgence of interest in pumpkins and squashes in Europe, especially in Britain, France, and Belgium, during the last decade.

## Folklore and fairy tales

Pùmpkins and squashes, perhaps because of their unusual and striking appearance, have always had a significant role in folklore. This is most vividly represented by the magic transformation of a pumpkin into a coach in the fairy tale Cinderella. The story, popularized in the West by French writer Charles Perrault, is thought to be of Eastern origin and was probably based on a nature myth in which Cinderella, representing the dawn, is oppressed by the night clouds (her cruel relatives) and saved by the sun (Prince Charming) — a delightful interpretation in which the magic pumpkin fits comfortably.

In other legends from around the world the pumpkin is often the central figure, usually taking on the role of protector and provider. Indian folklore, for example, tells of water, fish, whales, and entire rivers and oceans flowing from pumpkins. Other myths talk of pumpkins spouting precious oil, a year's supply of rice, and even treasures of silver and gold. Pumpkins have also been associated with rebirth, especially in Africa, Asia, and the Far East. In parts of Africa, tales abound of pumpkin plants springing up where people have died or have been buried.

Further west, though, especially in North America, stories center around reports of super-strong, vibrant pumpkins growing into the sky or across rivers, leading animals and humans astray. In New England and the South, where pumpkin growing is a way of life, similar reports can sometimes be heard.

Today, pumpkins are associated mainly with Halloween on October 31, the eve of All Hallows, which is the feast day of all the holy saints, known and unknown. This is also the beginning of the ancient Celtic New Year when traditionally the evil spirits of the previous year were frightened away by lighting great bonfires. Over the centuries these bonfires were abandoned and replaced by portable lanterns made from turnips (by the early colonists of America and by people from the north of England and Scotland) or pumpkins, which became more widely used in North America — a custom that has now crossed the Atlantic to Europe. It is still said that standing a jack-o'-lantern on the window ledge or by the door will keep evil spirits away.

Whatever the mythical powers of pumpkins and squashes, take time to grow them, enjoy their beauty, and savor their bountiful culinary qualities. Perhaps some of their legendary magic will be transferred to you. It has to me.

# in the garden

*Pumpkins and squashes are among the most rewarding plants to grow in the vegetable garden. Once established, the speed with which they grow is always surprising, but they can be trained and contained with little effort. They add visual interest to flower borders or climbing up over walls and fences.*

*The botanical classification of most pumpkins and squashes in cultivation is not complicated as the majority belong to three species of the same genus. It is only bottle gourds that fall into a separate genus.*

# Botanical Classification

O f all the groups in the vegetable kingdom, none can rival pumpkins and squashes for diversity of shape, size, and color. In shape they range from perfectly round and smooth to large, torpedo-shaped, and "warty." Sizes can vary from 2½ inches/ 6cm in diameter, weighing only a few ounces/grams, to 5 feet/1.5m in diameter, weighing over 1,000 pounds/450kg. And in color they range from creamy-white through yellow to deep orange-red, with all shades of green to black and metallic blues.

This spectrum of characteristics reflects the mixed and complex parentage of each cultivar (variety). Although there are few clear botanical distinctions between pumpkins and winter squash, they are grouped into categories making it possible to distinguish between those for culinary or decorative use.

For the sake of simplicity it is best to consider briefly the botanical classifications of pumpkins and squashes and then their horticultural groupings (*see* page 16). Understanding the botanical distinctions makes it easy to fit each plant into its correct species.

Pumpkins and squashes belong to the genus *Cucurbitaceae* and are related to cucumbers, melons, other gourds, and luffas. Surprisingly, the fruit is strictly speaking a berry; it is a simple fruit with pulpy flesh that does not split to reveal the seeds. They are monoecious: that is, they have separate male and female flowers on the same plant. The former are most numerous and can be distinguished by their long stem and single calyx; the latter have a much shorter stem with the fruit at the base of the flower. The female flower withers and drops off if it is not properly fertilized.

Most of the fruit described in this book belong to the genus *Cucurbita*. The only exception is *Lagenaria siceraria* (bottle gourd), which is particularly decorative and has been used for centuries in many countries to make vessels and musical instruments.

## Main groups

There are between 20 and 27 different species of *Cucurbita,* depending on which botanical authority you choose to follow. These include *C. mixta* (sometimes known as *C. argyrosperma*), the silver-seed gourd or cushaw, and *C. ficifolia*, the large malabar or fig-leaf gourd, *C. foetidissima*, the Missouri or Buffalo gourd, *C. texanana*, a native of Texas, and *C. sororia,* which all have small roundish fruit. However, the three main species of the genus, which represent the edible pumpkins and squashes are — *Cucurbita maxima, Cucurbita moschata,* and *Cucurbita pepo* — and they are most easily distinguished by looking at their fruit stems (peduncles). The species *C. maxima* havè large, corky or spongy stems, which are round and larger at the base (nearest the fruit). The stems of *C. moschata* are angled and fleshy, rather than rounded and ropy, opening out toward the fruit, becoming distinctively star-shaped and knobby. The stems of *C. pepo* are ridged all around, widening slightly at the base.

Due to the ease with which members of each species cross-pollinate, many of the older varieties that are open-pollinated, naturally, out in the field can be quite unstable. I have grown two plants from the same packet of 'Atlantic Giant' seeds that produced quite different fruit. One was the normal yellow-orange while the other was green. Another year I grew one fruit that I was never able to identify, as it resembled nothing I had sown. Less dramatically, there are slight variations between plants, as in the case of the colorful 'Turk's Turban', which can produce a perfectly formed "turban" with a huge "button," or a flatter specimen with a barely noticable lump.

The other consequence of the promiscuity of pumpkins and squashes is that it is difficult to save seed successfully from your own fruit, if you grow more than one variety in close proximity.

## Recent developments

Many of the cultivars available today from seed merchants have been in cultivation for more than a century (some of these were thought to have been lost but have recently been reintroduced). More importantly, new "$F_1$" cultivars are becoming available, particularly from North America. These represent the first generation ($F_1$) seed of a controlled cross in which the progeny have the characteristics of the parent with dominant genes. They have two major advantages over open-pollinated cultivars. The first is that they are reliably consistent, and the second is that they mature in a shorter period. They can, therefore, grow successfully in areas where the season is shorter and the summers cooler.

*All pumpkins and squashes fit into five groups. Knowing which one each*

*type of fruit belongs to makes it easier to choose the most suitable cultivar*

*for cooking or for decorating. It also helps to find them in seed catalogues.*

# Main Horticultural Groups

**Summer squashes** are all members of the species *pepo* and include zucchini (or courgettes), crooknecks, a number of round cultivars, and the pattypans or scallop squashes. These should all be picked for the kitchen when they are immature — the smaller the better. Both zucchini and pattypans come in a variety of colors, from palest creamy green to nearly black, and different shades of yellow. The flavors and textures, too, differ significantly.

If you allow the pattypans to grow to maturity, they become ornamentals, especially the white ones and the dark green 'Scallop Scallopini'.

**Autumn squashes** include members of the species *pepo* that are eaten when mature (i.e., during the fall), but not stored for more than two months. The most notable are acorn squash, which may be dark green, creamy white, or golden yellow.

Spaghetti squash is an oddity as its flesh comes away in large strands when cooked. It is egg-shaped and cultivars vary in color from creamy white to yellow to green-striped.

Last is the marrow (overgrown zucchini), virtually unknown in North America. It was once highly popular in the United Kingdom, but is now out of favor for being watery. It has a delicious, delicate flavor.

**Zucchini 'Mongo'**

**Spaghetti squash 'Pyjamas'**

**Hubbard squash 'New England Blue'**

**Winter squashes** in contrast to autumn squashes, have excellent keeping qualities (sometimes up to a year) and belong to the species *maxima* and *moschata*. Within this category are several distinct groups, including the butternuts, hubbards, kabouchas, sweet potatoes, buttons, and others. Their colors are enormously varied — red, pink, orange, yellow, white, gray-blue, dark green, and nearly black examples can all be found. Shape and size are equally mixed. Winter squashes can be smooth, warty, round, ribbed, pear- and torpedo-shaped. Sizes range from little two pounders (1kg) to robust 50 pounders (25kg). Winter squashes all have dense, dry flesh that is ideally suited to culinary uses. They also have a strong, distinctive flavor that stands well on its own, unlike the majority of pumpkins, which are more watery and have a grainier texture.

**Pumpkins** are characterized by a rounded shape and yellow to orange color. They belong mainly to the species *pepo*, but include a few *maxima*. Many start off green and turn orange toward the end of the growing season, but some have a yellow gene that ensures early coloring. As with the other horticultural categories, pumpkins display a range of characteristics; there are miniatures that weigh no more than a few ounces/125g, while the largest of the genus weigh nearly 1,000 pounds/500kg.

**Pumpkin 'Aspen'**

**Striped, warty skinned Pear gourd**

**Ornamental gourds** comprise the final horticultural group. These include the inedible *C. pepo* cultivars, which are all small and essentially pear-shaped or round and come with or without warts. They also come in a range of colors: cream, yellow, green, and orange are the most commonly found, but combinations of most of these hues add to the variety. There are also several edible cultivars of both *C. pepo* (the tiniest pumpkins such as the orange-colored 'Jack-be-Little' and the cream-colored 'Baby Boo') and *C. maxima* (particularly the Turk's Turban group) that have unusually eccentric shapes and are frequently grown for ornamental use. The final member of this horticultural group is *C. ficifolia*, the malabar or fig-leaf gourd, with its mottled green and cream ovoid fruit which, although edible, is not wonderfully tasty but makes an attractive decoration.

*While the fruits are growing, pumpkins and squashes provide good ground cover in the garden, helping to drive away weeds with their strong, attractive leaves and flowers.*

# Flowers, Leaves, & Seeds

### Flowers

All pumpkins and squashes have bright yellow flowers, that are plentiful and edible. Usually, the bigger the fruit, the bigger the flower. If you come across white flowers in a *cucurbit* patch, they belong to the bottle gourd, *Lagenaria siceraria*, a welcome and attractive change.

### Leaves

At first glance the leaves of pumpkins and squashes appear to be similar, but there are specific differences that point to the plant's ancestry. *C. maxima* has circular or kidney-shaped leaves with shallow lobes and lightly ruffled edges. *C. moschata* has broad, heart-shaped leaves with five lobes, the top one being the largest. They are colored gray-green to cream — an attractive feature. The leaves of *C. pepo* are triangular with five deep lobes and serrated edges. A few have gray-green markings, others are solid dark green or yellow-green. *C. ficifolia* has leaves which,

A summer squash Ronde de Nice plant shows distinctive leaf markings. The male flowers have long stalks, but the fruit is at the base of the female flower.

**Cucurbita pepo**

Zucchini　　Ronde de Nice　　Jack-be-Little

**Naked seed**

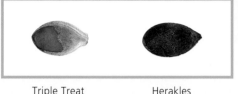

Triple Treat　　Herakles

**Cucurbita moschata**

Butternut　　Muscade de Provence

as its name suggests, are fig-leaf shaped with seven lobes, the three central ones being most pronounced.

Additionally, all leaves have long stalks, which make them stand up like huge plates, but beware: many are prickly (particularly cultivars of *C. maxima* and *C. pepo*) and may scratch your hands. There are a number of spineless cultivars, particularly of zucchini, which may be worth looking out for if you have sensitive skin. The spines can also damage young fruit if the wind blows a leaf across the tender skin.

## Seeds
Pumpkin and squash seeds are all essentially oval-shaped with one end slightly more pointed than the other. Some seeds may be

more rounded, others longer, but variations in size, color, and markings can also indicate their particular species.

The seeds of *C. pepo* are all smooth and come in shades of beige from light to dark. The smallest belong to zucchini, summer squashes, and tiny pumpkins, such as 'Jack-be-Little', and are slightly larger than the seed of cucumber and melons, but with a more clearly defined, paler margin (edge).

As a general rule, the larger the fruit, the bigger the seed. Not all seeds of cultivars, however, have the protective beige husk; they are called naked seed and are olive green in color. They have the advantage that they do not need shelling before being eaten; the disadvantage, though, is that they are more prone to rotting if the conditions

are not right for quick germination. Among the cultivars to have naked seed are 'Triple Treat' and 'Herakles'.

The seed of *C. moschata* is very alike: beige in color, but with a thin, ragged margin. *C. maxima* has the most attractive seed: some are beautiful, shiny tan with a pale margin, and some pure white with white margins, a marked contrast to *C. ficifolia*, which has black seed.

Finally, there is the silver-seeded gourd *C. mixta*, also known as *C. argyrosperma*, which includes the cushaw. These have a large white seed with a wide silvery, grayish, or bluish margin, and are over an inch/2½cm long.

Most pumpkin and squash seed are easy to handle and keep well for up to six years, or even longer if properly handled.

**Cucurbita maxima**

Chestnut　　Queensland Blue

**Cucurbita ficifolia**

Fig Leaf Gourd

**Cucurbita mixta**

Striped Cushaw

*Pumpkins and squashes are easy to grow, provided they have enough*

*heat, light, water, and nutrients. Plant them after the final spring frost.*

*They can be harvested right through summer until the first autumn frosts.*

# Growing Your Own
# Pumpkins & Squashes

**1.** During the spring prepare the soil by incorporating as much farmyard manure or compost as you can. If you want to get the soil really warm before planting (this encourages germination), cover it with a sheet of black plastic. This will also stop weeds from growing and will conserve moisture.

A well established pumpkin plant.

**2.** If you live in an area where there are late frosts, sow two seeds in a 3- inch/8-cm pot filled with potting mix about one month before the last frost is expected. Leave in a warm place (65° F/22° C) to germinate. This may take from five days to two weeks, or more if the temperature is not high enough.

**3**. In warmer areas, when all risk of frost has passed and the soil is beginning to warm up, sow two or three seeds in a small depression at regular intervals. The spacing between each group of seeds should be 1½-2 feet/45-60cm for summer squashes, 2-3 feet/60-90cm for pumpkins, winter squashes, and gourds. The rows should be 3 feet/90cm apart.

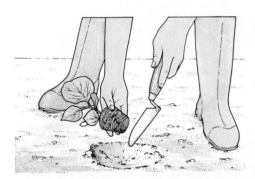

**4.** When all the plants are about 4 inches/10cm tall and four or five true leaves have grown, thin them by retaining the strongest plant. Keep the plants watered if there is no rain, and remove any weeds. Cover with a good mulch or a sheet of black plastic. If you are raising plants in pots, harden them off a few days as soon as any risk of frost has passed before planting out in the ground. Water them in well. Protect all young plants from slugs (see page 24).

**5.** As the plant grows, guide it within its allocated space by pinning down the stems, burying them under the soil at regular intervals. Roots will form along the stems and should be encouraged to grow into the ground if this is not happening naturally; these additional roots significantly help the plant to absorb water and nutrients.

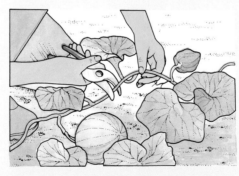

**6.** When the plant has filled its allocated space and fruit has set, cut any excessive growth back. If growing for size, thin the fruits to just two or three (see page 27). Once they are growing strongly, remove any newly set fruit. Usually the plant will do its own selection, allowing certain fruit to take precedence while others stop growing or rot off, remove these immediately.

**7.** Look out for mildew and any viral infection (see page 24). If possible, spray with fungicide to control the mildew; this allows maximum photosynthesis to continue to take place. Remove and dispose of any plant that shows signs of virus.

**8.** Zucchini should be harvested when 4-8 inches/10-20cm long. The more you pick, the more fruit will be produced. Leave the pumpkins and winter squashes to mature on the vine for as long as possible. To ripen, cut and leave on the ground for a week before bringing them in. If there is a threat of early frost and the fruits are exposed, cover them with a polyspun garden blanket (such as REMAY), sack, blanket, or newspaper, but harvest immediately after. They can then be stored in a dry, well-ventilated, frost-free spot where they will continue to ripen and will keep for several months.

*Pumpkins and squashes can be planted in a variety of ways in the garden: whether in the vegetable garden or in a flowerbed they can be used to cover the ground or grow over pergolas and fences.*

# Where to Plant Pumpkins & Squashes

All pumpkins and squashes need to grow successfully is a warm, open, sunny position that is comfortably sheltered from the wind. Well-drained, fertile soil will ensure that they grow particularly well, but they are remarkably tolerant of a variety of soils. As long as conditions are sufficiently warm and water and nutrients can be supplemented if necessary throughout the growingseason, pumpkins and squashes will grow with ease.

Most cultivars can be grown in many different sites in the garden, even if space is limited; only giant pumpkins require large areas. The most obvious place for bush, semi-bush, and smaller trailing cultivars is the vegetable garden, but many could be grown equally well in flowerbeds as an unusual but attractive filler. The bush zucchini, most summer squashes, and the winter squash 'Gold Nugget' are good, compact plants that can add a touch of the exotic to a border with their large, trumpet-shaped, bright yellow flowers and enormous palmate leaves. Even among the large Halloween pumpkins, there are some varieties that are reasonably compact, such as the open-pollinated 'Aspen'. This is a semi-bush variety and has only one or two stems that branch out from the center of the plant.

The smaller pumpkins such as 'Baby Bear' and Spooktacular and the miniature cultivars such as 'Sweetie Pie', 'Baby Boo', and 'Jack-be-Little' can all be grown very

easily in a small vegetable garden and produce fruit in reasonable quantities.

Up to five different cultivars of pumpkins and winter squashes can be grown successfully on a 6- by 12-foot/2- by 4-meter patch yielding at least ten fruits (often more). This would be an adequate crop for most families. Guide overenthusiastic stems back onto the plot until the ground is covered and then prune back any stems that start to overstep their mark.

## Training

Pumpkins and squashes can make effective, fast-growing screens through the summer if trained up a trellis or wire structure or over an arcade or arbor. Choose vigorous vining cultivars with small fruit, such as squashes 'Rolet' and 'Little Gem', mini-pumpkin 'Munchkin', winter squashes 'Baby Delica' and butternut, or ornamental gourds.

The white-flowered bottle gourd *Lagenaria siceraria* is a particularly decorative candidate for screening purposes. Excluding the largest *Lagenaria* fruit, which will need the support of nets, it is surprising how strong the stems of bottle gourds of all shapes can be. They will withstand endless pushing and shoving without showing any signs of strain on their stems. The advantage of growing these gourds over a support is that they are able to develop good, straight fruit whereas if grown on the ground, they tend to twist. The snake gourd, for example, takes on a serpentine appearance when grown on the ground, but when trained over a raised structure, produces straight fruit as the effect of gravity stretches it out.

Training pumpkins and squashes along the chosen wall or fence is not as difficult as it may initially seem. A little guidance will be necessary at the beginning, but the plant's long tendrils quickly grip onto wire, string, or other plants, and its hollow stems weave easily through the support. Some pruning may be needed to contain the growth. One word of warning: Make sure the supporting structure is solid and secure enough to carry the weight of the foliage and fruit, or it may tumble down just as the display is reaching its height.

Above The diversity of shape and small size of ornamental gourds make them ideal for growing over an iron structure.

Left The colorful flowers and fruit of gourds add interest to a wooden fence during the summer.

*There are few pests and diseases that affect pumpkins and squashes,*

*especially when successfully cultivated in the garden. However, beware,*

*there are a few foes that may be encountered.*

# Pests & Diseases

## Pests

The main pest to threaten pumpkins and squashes is the mouse. To these little rodents, the seed is like manna from heaven. Even if you have sown seeds in pots in a greenhouse, repeated nocturnal visits from these pests will guarantee that you never succeed in germinating, let alone growing, plants.

If you do not want to use poison or mousetraps and you don't have a cat, bring the pots into the house and place them on a window sill until they can be put out in the ground. Mice may reappear at the end of the season to nibble at the ripening fruit, but all they will do is damage the fruit, rather than destroy it altogether.

After planting seedlings in the garden, slugs are the next danger. To stop them from eating your new seedlings, place slug pellets, bowls of beer, or broken eggshells around them, as a mode of defense.

Further into the growing cycle, aphids may be found feeding on the plants and should be controlled, not so much for the damage they themselves do, but because they are vectors for cucumber mosaic virus (CMV). Aphids generally feed on plants that are already stressed through lack of water or nutrients and are therefore most vulnerable.

The greatest threats to plants in hotter climates are pumpkin and striped cucumber beetles which, if they infest in the early part of the season, can easily destroy small plants. They feed on the leaves, flowers, and even young fruit. Vine borers, another pest which literally bores into the stems, may also cause trouble later.

All these pests should be controlled with a general-purpose garden insecticide. Cultivars of *C. moschata* are most resistant to viral disease and pests.

## Diseases

Cucumber mosaic virus and powdery mildew are the major diseases to watch for. CMV causes the leaves to become crinkled, misshapen, and mottled yellow. The plant also becomes stunted and often collapses. This serious disease of the *cucurbit* family can only be controlled by destroying any affected plants. To prevent the disease from spreading, make sure your hands and any tools that you have used are cleaned thoroughly before they come into contact with other plants.

Powdery mildew must be controlled from the beginning of the season as it inhibits photosynthesis and reduces the quality of the crop. Later in the season, it can cause the fruit to rot once picked. Commercial growers spray early with fungicide as a preventative measure against this destructive disease.

In the garden, spray only if the first sign — gray, powdery fungus — appears on the leaves and spreads to the stems. Contact fungicide is the recommended remedy and best used when the plant is most vulnerable to the disease — when it is stressed due to lack of water or when the conditions are cool and damp, such as in early fall. Alternatively, spray as soon as the powdery patches appear, and then every ten days. Keeping the plants well irrigated and removing and destroying plants at the end of the season will help prevent recurrence.

**Above** The distinctive gray mouldy patches of powdery mildew will spread to cover the whole leaf of a *cucurbit* and severely impede photosynthesis.

**Left** Cucumber mosaic virus is a serious disease that may attack most *cucurbits*, causing stunting followed by collapse of the plant. It should be controlled by removing and burning the affected plant. It is spread by contact and aphids flying from plant to plant.

*For the first time in 1996, at least two pumpkins exceeded a half ton.*

*Other statistics associated with world champions are no less staggering:*

*14-foot circumferences and growth rates of as many as 10 inches per day.*

# Giant Pumpkins

That pumpkins and squashes have the capacity to grow to enormous sizes is both their downfall and their glory. Tough, tasteless, watery flesh is associated with the largest fruit and this puts anyone off from growing them for cooking. But one has to admire those for whom growing for size is as much a passion as growing a great collection of different varieties is for others.

The growing techniques used are fascinating. For, while growing 'Atlantic Giant' to a modest 60 pounds/30kg is possible with relatively little attention and care, devoted preparation and cosseting throughout the growing season is required for champions, which frequently reach 800 pounds/360kg or more; the staggering world record in 1996 stands at 1,061 pounds/481kg.

## Growing giant pumpkins

With a little dedication, it is possible to grow spectacular, giant pumpkins. Simply follow these few instructions:

**1.** First prepare the ground by digging a pit 3 x 3 x 3 feet/1 x 1 x 1 meters and backfilling it with some well-rotted farm manure mixed with the original soil. Then cover the patch with black plastic to warm it up and conserve the moisture.

**2.** Meanwhile, sow the seed about two to three weeks before the last predicted frost. Once it has two true leaves, plant it out. The art is then to feed it with the correct combination of fertilizers. For example, a grower might for the first few weeks apply a fertilizer rich in phosphate for strong root growth. This would be followed by a balanced fertilizer to encourage all-round growth of roots, leaves, and flowers, while applying a potash-rich foliar feed to ensure good formation of the embryo pumpkins.

**3.** Once two types of flowers are on the plant (the sign that cross-pollination has taken place), revert to high phosphate fertilizer to push root growth. When the fruit has set successfully, the all-round fertilizer can be used, applied to both soil and foliage. Frequent, generous watering is vital.

**4.** When the nights get cooler, put a cover over the pumpkin to conserve the heat. If it is rainy or windy, a little shelter break should be constructed to minimize any damage. The art lies in keeping the plant growing, without check, for as long as possible.

Giant pumpkin growing is a highly competitive business. Seed is carefully selected from the biggest specimens; Howard Dill of Nova Scotia (far left), who won the world record four times from 1979 to 1982, has been at the forefront of the distribution of some of the best seed. These gargantuan gourds need several men and machinery (left) to harvest and move them from growing site to scales. William Greer (top) of Pickton, Ontario broke the "unbreakable" 1,000 pound/455kg barrier on October 5, 1996. He held the world title for just an hour as the pumpkin Nathan and Paula Zehr (above) had spent a total of 900 manhours nurturing weighed in at 1,061 pounds/482kg in Clarence, New York.

27

*The range of different cultivars grown commercially is limited, but they are a useful crop for farmers being easy to produce — if a little labor intensive at harvest time — often resulting in a pick-your-own policy.*

# Commercial Growing

The sight of a field of ripening pumpkins when driving along a country road is quite breathtaking. After the first light frost, when the canopy of leaves has dropped and the trees are just beginning to assume their autumnal tints, the fruit shines in the low light like bright orange jewels for acre upon acre. This is a familiar sight in parts of North America, one that heralds the beginning of the festive season that starts at Halloween and lasts right up to the New Year.

Traditionally pumpkins and squashes are regarded as low-maintenance crops for farmers, which can be sown and more or less left until the harvest. But, as with many things undertaken by professionals, much experimentation and experience goes into achieving the best return on the crop with the lowest possible expenditure. With commercial growing there is no space for mistakes, which are costly.

In most of the pumpkin-growing areas of the United States, the season is reliably warm, so it is possible to sow seed directly in the field when there is enough moisture for the seed to germinate. In parts of Canada and Europe, pumpkins, squashes, and ornamental gourds tend to be sown in flats, pots, or modules three to four weeks before they are transplanted into warm earth. The art is to time it just right so that the seedlings can be planted out as soon as they have filled their tiny indoor growing space. If the weather is going against the grower, then careful watering and feeding keep the plants in good condition.

Most commercial growers only spray the young plants once in order to control weeds. This takes place when the plants are compact enough to allow a tractor through the rows. This is also the time when a protective spray against powdery mildew can be used; two or three applications at two- to three-week intervals usually provide good protection until the end of the season.

At harvest time, if the fruit has not had time to cure (when the skins harden and the stems seal), the vine is cut and the fruit left in the field. Then the farmer hopes for a warm, dry spell (ideally, ten days at 77° F/ 25° C) to cure the fruits completely. After harvesting, which is done by hand, pumpkins and squashes are stored indoors before being taken to market.

**Right** The spectacular sight of a commercially grown pumpkin field in Half Moon Bay, south of San Francisco, California. The foliage has been removed to allow the fruit to ripen fully.

# around the home

*Pumpkins, squashes, and gourds are beautiful to look at in their own right and an asset in any artistic arrangement, but with imagination and a few tools they can be turned into magnificent decorative objects. On the following pages are some projects that touch upon the creative possibilities. They include carving, decorating, painting, flower displays, and seed work.*

*By their very nature most of these projects are bound to perish, but perhaps this ephemeral and seasonal quality is one of their attractions. Do take photographs as keepsakes, particularly of the pieces you are most proud of.*

# Halloween "Jack-O'-Lantern"

1 large pumpkin

Soft pencil or felt-tip pen

Strong kitchen knife

Craft knife or pumpkin-carving kit

Melon baller or strong metal spoon

Metal skewer

Selection of leaves, twigs, and berries
with strong stems

Short thick candle with holder

Pumpkins have been used in North America for carving jack-o'-lanterns for as long as anyone can remember, but in Europe they are a recent addition to Halloween festivities.

Select a pumpkin to suit the design, incorporating any asymmetry, lumps, and bumps, and eradicating any blemishes. Make sure that it is not badly bruised and the stem (often referred to as the handle) is firmly attached. If it is not — rot is setting in.

Decide what expression to draw: a happy, sad, fierce, or ghoulish face with a big or small mouth, short or long nose, eyebrows, and wrinkles, and use as much of the pumpkin surface as possible.

The tools used should be sharp, so be careful, especially when supervising children. Use care when lighting the jack-o'-lantern, too. Be sure that it is away from flammable objects and that the candle is secure.

Two to five days is the average life of a lantern as the heat of the candle dehydrates and shrinks the pumpkin. Try standing it in water for a short while to rehydrate it and keep it in a cool place at night.

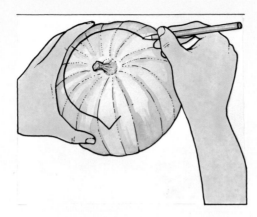

**1.** Prepare the pumpkin for carving: Examine the pumpkin for blemishes or misshapen surfaces and choose which side of the pumpkin you will carve. Mark the lid, including a V-shaped notch at the back to allow you to replace the lid easily and to give a close fit.

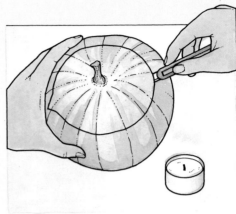

**2.** Next cut out the lid, making sure the knife is kept at an angle. Always cut away from your hand, rotating the pumpkin as necessary. Remove the strings and seeds from inside, leaving a hollow shell. With the melon baller, scrape away the pulp from the area you will be carving until the pumpkin is approximately 1 inch/2½ cm thick.

**3.** Draw your design on the pumpkin using a soft pencil or a felt-tip pen. When you are happy with the design, with the skewer prick the lines of the design; this will help you to control the carving. Place the pumpkin on a flat work surface. Carve your pattern, removing the flesh to be discarded by pushing out the shapes from the inside of the pumpkin.

**4.** When you have completed the carving, make holes with the skewer in the lid and the back of the pumpkin and push in decorative leaves, twigs, and berries. Add the candle, making sure that it is stable before you light it.

# Jeweled Pumpkin

1 large pumpkin

Dressmaking or glass-headed pins

Selection of cookie cutters

Small hammer

Strong kitchen knife

Melon baller or strong metal spoon

Craft knife or pumpkin-carving kit

Selection of beads, braids, sequins, ribbon

Short, thick candle with holder

Cinderella's fairy godmother could have had a hand in decorating this sequined lantern; or could it have been Fabergé, pausing between eggs? Whoever it was, this sophisticated design is surprisingly simple to realize. It makes a spectacular alternative, or complement, to the more traditionally sculpted examples. While I used a white-skinned 'Lumina' pumpkin, the classic orange-skinned varieties also yield lovely results.

The method introduces a unique and easy way to achieve a regular repeat pattern on your pumpkin, using a small hammer and a cookie cutter as a guide.

Mark the pattern before you start; this can easily be done with pins. The number of repeats depends on the pumpkin's size.

The steps for preparation are similar to that for the jack-o'-lantern (*see* page 33), but only done once the design has been hammered into the skin.

Safety is the essential consideration when carving the pattern and inserting pins. Always supervise children and make sure that the candle is secure and the pumpkin is away from any flammable materials.

**1.** Using pins, mark the pattern repeats around your pumpkin; the number will depend on the size of your cookie cutter. Hammer the cookie cutter into the flesh to a depth of approximately ½ inch/1¼ cm. Remove and repeat the process until the pattern is complete.

**2.** Cut out the lid, and remove the strings and seeds as described in steps 1 and 2 *Halloween Jack-O'Lantern* on page 33. In this instance, you will have to remove the flesh of the entire fruit to a depth of 1 inch/2½ cm, as the pattern covers the entire surface.

**3.** Finish carving out the pattern, using a sharp knife. Remove the surplus flesh by pushing out the shapes from the inside of the pumpkin. With the knife tidy the outlines of the pattern repeats you have created with the cookie cutter.

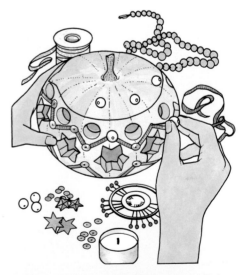

**4.** When you have completed the carving, add the braid or ribbon in patterns of your choice, attaching it to the pumpkin with the glass-headed pins. Finally, decorate with beads threaded onto pins and pushed firmly into the flesh. Add the candle, making sure it is stable before you light it.

# Carved Pumpkins & Squashes

1 pumpkin or squash

Linoleum cutter and various sized nibs or
wood-cutting tools

Tracing paper (optional)

Tape (optional)

Dressmaking pins (optional)

Soft pencil (optional)

Cookie cutters (optional)

Small hammer (optional)

Food coloring (optional)

Small artist's paintbrush (optional)

If you want to avoid all the preparation
required to make a jack-o'-lantern, pumpkin-
carving is a highly satisfying alternative. The
creative scope is endless. From something
simple and freehand to an extremely ornate
and complicated exhibition piece, it can
provide hours of fun. With a carved pumpkin
there is also much less dehydration than
occurs with a jack-o'-lantern, so the finished
piece lasts a lot longer.

You can sketch your design on paper, then
redraw it on the pumpkin using a soft pencil;
draw a freehand design (*see* photo); or try the
hammer and cookie cutter technique used in
the Jeweled Pumpkin (*see* page 35), creating
outlines from which to work.

When selecting your pumpkin or squash,
look for one with a fairly firm, smooth skin.
The design can be even more effective if you
find one with skin a different color from the
flesh, such as a blue or green squash.
Alternatively, the use of contrasting food
colorings will emphasize the pattern created.

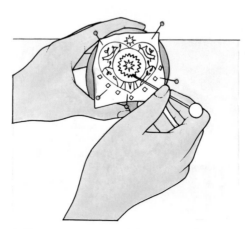

**1.** If you want to try your design on paper first, use
tracing paper which will be easy to wrap around the
pumpkin. To transfer the design, tape or pin the
paper around the pumpkin or squash and prick the
pattern through it using a hat pin or dressmaking
pins. Remove the paper pattern, and, if you need to,
join the dots using a soft pencil.

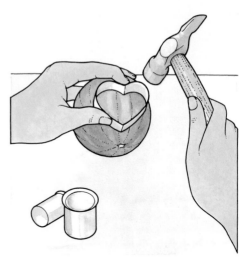

**2.** The cookie cutter method is the same as
described in the jeweled pumpkin project (*see* page
35), but you do not need to hammer it in as deeply.
Avoid using a large cookie cutter as you may find it
difficult to apply the pattern on the curve of the
pumpkin or squash.

**3.** Using the linoleum cutter or wood-cutting tools,
carve the skin to the pattern desired. Remember,
always cut away from your hands.

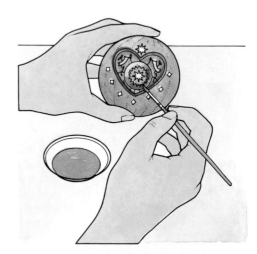

**4.** If you would like to add some extra color to your
pumpkin or squash, mix food coloring with a little
water. Paint the color roughly into the carved design
with a small paintbrush. Any excess that gets onto
the skin can be wiped off with a paper towel.

# Miniature Pomanders

A selection of ornamental gourds or pumpkins
  (such as 'Baby Boo' or 'Jack-be-Little')
Decorative ribbon
Thumbtacks
Selection of spices –
  cinnamon sticks, fresh rosemary sprigs,
  cloves, fresh or freshly dried bay, sage,
  or other aromatic leaves, ground nutmeg,
  pumpkin pie spice mix
Metal skewer
Dressmaking pins
Craft knife
Essential oils – orange and lemon

Some 25 years ago, a friend gave me a
pomander made from an orange stuck with
cloves and wrapped in a piece of orange
gingham tied with a silky piece of apricot-
colored ribbon. I still have the pomander.
The gingham and ribbon are a little faded,
but the scent retains its magic.

It has served as an inspiration for these
decorative gourds and mini-pumpkins. Each
one is the perfect vehicle for its own aromatic
spice or oil and the added fragrance makes
them all the more appealing for display.

These pomanders are quick and easy to
make. The only tricky bit is tying the ribbon,
but using thumbtacks to secure the ribbon
while you tie it makes the task a lot easier.

Hang these around the house in groups,
for example, from a window frame — or
offer them as gifts for the Thanksgiving
table. A word of warning: Be careful not to
get the oils or spices in your eyes. They can
also leave marks on clothes or walls, so
position your pomanders carefully.

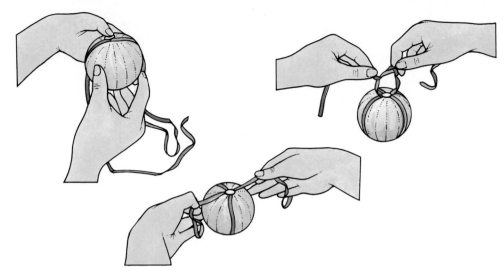

**1.** Take at least 24 inches/70cm of ribbon. Bring the
ends together and attach the middle of the ribbon to
the top of the gourd or pumpkin with a thumbtack.
Bring the two ends around and tie them in a knot at
the bottom. (Depending how flat the base of the gourd or pumpkin is, you may need to anchor the
knot with a thumbtack as well.) Bring the two free
ends to the top again, slip them under the already
secured ribbon — one on each side — and tie them
in a knot.

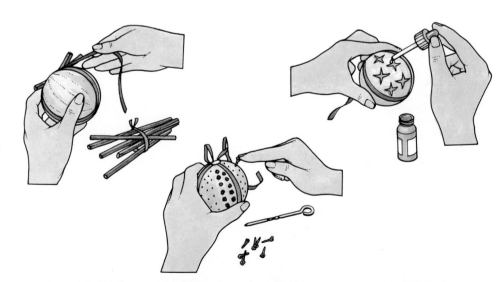

**2.** Now you can start adding the aromatics —
I recommend that you use only one scent per item.
Tie the cinnamon sticks or the rosemary sprigs on
top with the excess ribbon. Or make holes in the
flesh with the skewer, then push in cloves all over
— be warned, some of them can be sharp. Using
dressmaking pins, secure the bay or sage leaves
to the top and bottom of the pumpkin. If using freshly dried leaves, mist or steam them, if
necessary, so that they are flexible enough not to
crack or break. Finally, on some of your pomanders,
cut small incisions into the flesh in an informal
decorative pattern and while the flesh is still wet,
rub in some ground nutmeg or pumpkin pie spice
mix, or drip on some essential oil. Add a decorative
bow to finish the pomander.

# Floral Thanksgiving Display

3 pumpkins, 1 large and 2 small
Strong kitchen knife
Craft knife
Florist's foam, soaked in water
  (follow manufacturer's instructions)
8 tall candles, various lengths
Selection of seasonal flowers and trailing greenery
Thin curling ribbon
Scissors

The natural combination of flowers and greenery tumbling out of a plump, ripe pumpkin epitomizes autumn, harvest, and, of course, Thanksgiving. These arrangements add color, warmth, and style to any dining room and are fun to make, too.

This display works well in a variety of places, but if it is for a table centerpiece, make sure that the pumpkins are not too big, as you will have difficulty seeing your guests or have no room for the plates.

You could also make a little display for each place setting, using tiny pumpkins such as 'Baby Boo' and/or 'Jack-be-Little', alternating them to achieve an orange-and-white effect. The guests' names could be written on little flags attached to ribbons or green wires and stuck among the greenery.

Remember to choose a tablecloth that suits the general color scheme and complements and enhances your arrangements. Pumpkins always lose a certain amount of moisture, which could ruin good furniture surfaces, so set them on a tray or a plate before positioning them.

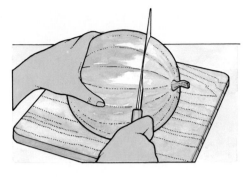

**1.** Find a pumpkin with a good stable base and no holes in the skin. Cut approximately one third off the top of the pumpkin.

**2.** Remove seeds and strings, then carve a zigzag pattern around the top edge, ½ inch/1¼ cm deep to help the flowers sit around the top of the pumpkin.

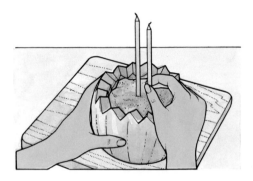

**3.** Cut away the pulp from the top opening, then pack the pumpkin with the prepared florist's foam. Position the candles by pushing them into the florist's foam.

**4.** Next position three or four large flowers for structure. Arrange the smaller flowers, pushing them into the foam. Start from the outer edge of the pumpkin and work toward the center.

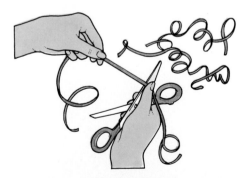

**5.** Create each ribbon tendril by pulling a piece of ribbon along the blade of a pair of scissors, making sure that the natural curl of the ribbon is face down on the scissors. If this process does not automatically create a curl, try turning the ribbon over and pulling it again.

**6.** Repeat the process using the small pumpkins. Use smaller flowers and candles. Once the flower arrangements are complete, position the pumpkins, placing the smaller ones near the large display and decorate with tendrils of greenery and ribbon.

Materials used in
pictured swag :

pattypans
pumpkins
gourds
hops
eucalyptus
poppy heads
wheat stalks
assorted dried flowers
seed pods

# Festive Swag

Wire cutters

Chicken wire, 1 inch/2½ cm gauge

Florist's foam (gray, dry type)

Gardening gloves (or other protective gloves)

A selection of pattypans, pumpkins, gourds,
    tamarillo, moss, ivy, grains, Indian corn,
    hops, Chinese lanterns, eucalyptus,
    seed pods, red chilies, dried flowers, nuts

Medium- and heavy-gauge florist wire (stub wire)

Craft knife

A festive mantel, door, or wall decoration of natural flowers and vegetables can be especially eye-catching when it includes gourds of different shapes and colors. But supporting the weight of all these items is often a problem, with a gourd here or a pod there periodically dropping off!

This method uses a solid "sausage" of chicken wire wrapped around florist's foam as the core and anchor of the arrangement. The pumpkins, gourds, and other heavier items are wired onto the chicken-wire base, while flowers are simply pushed into the foam.

Using this base, you can create a variety of shapes to suit different locations — swags for long mantelpieces and door jambs, or wall hangings for hall, kitchen, or dining room.

What you include is entirely your choice. You could continue the gourd colors (yellow, orange, green, and white) in the foliage that you choose, or be daring and mix a little of everything for a cheerful riot of color.

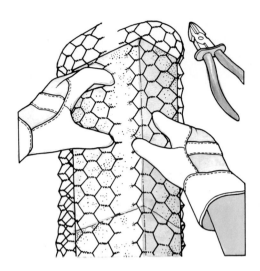

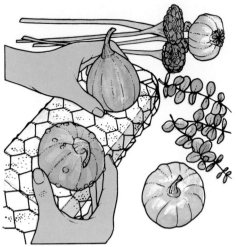

**1.** Use a piece of string to calculate the length of your swag. With wire cutters, cut a length of chicken wire, lay it flat, and place the blocks of dry florist's foam in the center — they may need to be cut to fit your requirements. Wearing the gardening gloves, wrap the wire around the foam to make a tube, taking care to push in all the sharp ends.

**2.** Gather your materials together, separating the heavier items like baby pumpkins, gourds, and Indian corn. These will need to be attached with wire, and should be arranged first in order to act as focal points in the display. Work *in situ,* if possible, so that you can keep an eye on both the weight and scale of the arrangement.

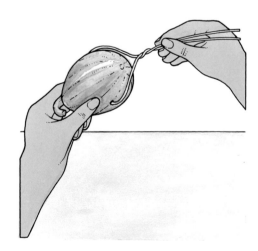

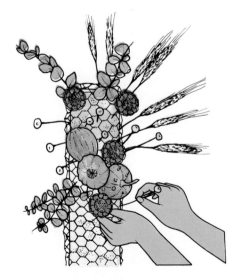

**3.** To wire the heavy items, you will need to pierce them, probably in two places, and then thread heavy-gauge florist wire through the holes and twist. The items can then be securely wired to the chicken-wire frame.

**4.** Working from the center out, position your flowers, grains, and vegetables in whatever combination you wish by pushing their stems or supporting wires into the florist's foam. Do this until the arrangement is complete.

# Pumpkin-Seed Patchwork Box

A square box — wooden or heavy cardboard with
   a removable lid
Latex paint
Brush
Sandpaper, fine
2 gift-wrap papers, one plain, one patterned
Craft knife
Metal ruler
Wallpaper paste
Dried pumpkin seeds
White craft glue
Clear varnish

These lacquered boxes will hold jewelry, cuff
links, buttons, or other small items that can
clutter up surfaces or be easily lost. They are
cheerful additions to any dresser or side-
board and make special personalized gifts.

You can use any size box, but you may
want to experiment with a small one first.
You can use bigger or smaller seeds (from
different sorts of pumpkins and squashes)
depending on the size of the box, or a
combination of small and large seeds to
give more texture. The secret of success in
all cases, though, is patience! Take time to
measure box and paper carefully before you
start, and make sure each layer of paint and
varnish dries thoroughly before you
progress to the next stage.

To dry pumpkin or squash seeds, rinse
with cold water and pat dry with paper
towels. Transfer to a flat open container
and let dry naturally in a warm, dry place
for about a week.

**1.** Apply a coat of paint to the visible surfaces of the box and let it dry thoroughly. When dry, smooth the box with fine sandpaper, apply another coat of paint, and let it dry. Then, paint the bottom of the box, letting it dry completely as well.

**2.** Create the pattern for the lid: Place the lid on wrong side of gift wrap and trace around it. Measure length and width of the paper and divide into equal squares (minimum 16). Cut out squares using craft knife and metal ruler. Eight will be used for the lid.

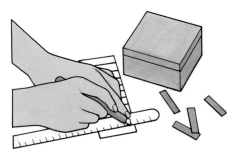

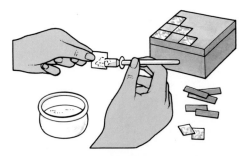

**3.** Measure two sides of your box for length and depth, then mark the dimensions on the wrong side of the second, contrasting piece of gift wrap. Divide the paper into at least 16 strips of equal width, mark, and cut out.

**4.** Glue the eight squares of paper to the lid of the box in a patchwork pattern with wallpaper paste (this allows you to move them into place), making sure that all the edges of the paper are secured. Replace the lid.

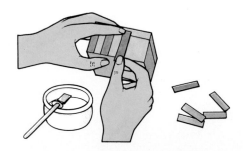

**5.** To create the stripe pattern, glue the paper strips to the sides, spacing them equally around the whole box, and over the seam between lid and box. When dry, carefully cut through the strips using a sharp craft knife. The lid can now be removed.

**6.** Arrange pumpkin seeds in flower patterns on top of the box, gluing them with craft glue. Let the whole box dry thoroughly, then apply four coats of varnish. Let each coat dry thoroughly before applying the next.

# Ornamental Gourds

In the fall bowls of pumpkins, squashes, and gourds are colorful and decorative accents. Unfortunately, pumpkins and squashes start to rot after a few months, while most gourds slowly dry out and turn a pale straw color. Some gourds keep their full, rounded, or warty shape, while others wizen a little. Those gourds that have not matured on the vine, or have been bruised, tend to rot before they dry out and should be discarded to prevent soggy messes on the furniture.

There are, however, several ways of prolonging and enhancing the decorative qualitites of ornamental gourds. Most frequently they are varnished or waxed, which makes them shine and enhances their natural colors. Alternatively, they can be painted with gold and silver for a really bright display, or with other colors to blend in more subtly with the general color scheme.

In the picture at left, a gourd has been painted all over with red acrylic paint in a repeating pattern (in this case an exaggerated "C" shape, with little feathery additions; a simple flower outline would work equally well). Once the red paint had dried thoroughly, the gourd was bronzed. To make a thin bronzing or silvering wash, mix a small amount of gold or silver powder paint with craft glue and thinly apply all over the gourd.

Another interesting idea is to paint a geometric design reminiscent of the decorations on African tribal vessels or Native North American baskets or a freestyle design directly onto the gourds. Such patterns can make use of the natural shape and markings of the gourds, each one different from the others. The display is held together by the strong black line decoration.

Remember that the choice of container will significantly alter the tone of any display of decorated pumpkins and gourds. The combinations are endless: The look will be essentially rustic if a wooden or earthenware bowl is used, or more sophisticated if a ceramic dish is chosen. A touch of the Oriental can be achieved by using some Chinese rice dishes. Be generous and pile the pumpkins and gourds high for a sense of abundance, or select a small number of the most beautiful for a simpler, more minimalist approach.

These contemporary Peruvian scribed gourds show the craft at it's most intricate.

# Other Uses

**Above** Bottle gourds, due to their extraordinary shapes, lend themselves to a variety of different uses. Most frequently, they are hollowed out and used as containers, like the engraved example above.

**Right** This birdhouse made using gourds is a fine example of how stunning these fruit can be when put to such imaginative use.

In the previous pages I have detailed some examples of projects that can be carried out at home; however, there is no end to the creative ways pumpkins and gourds can be used. It is always fun, for example, to carve a pattern or message onto a young squash or pumpkin on the vine and watch it grow with the fruit. As a scar, it becomes a permanent decorative feature of the squash or pumpkin.

Seeds can be pressed into service to create beautiful pictures and collages using different sizes and colors to give depth and texture to the image. Pencil, paint, and fabric will complete the work if necessary and differences in seed sizes are very useful, for example, when making necklaces. This can be done simply by using a needle and thread. Finally, pumpkins and squashes are wonderful subjects for paintings, tapestries, and appliqué work.

Some of the finest craftsmanship has been practiced on gourds (*Lagenaria siceraria*) throughout Africa, India, China, and the Americas for many centuries. The different shapes and forms of gourds lend themselves to a diversity of uses. Items made from gourds have traditionally been decorated according to their function, and many are still in use to this day.

Variously shaped gourds can be used as bottles. The most common shape has a long neck and broad base, while the pilgrim's gourd is bilobed (vaguely hourglass-shaped) and only about 8 inches/20cm tall; the little flat Corsican gourd is used more as a hip flask. Straps made from hemp or agave fiber are often knotted around the bulb to carry them.

Among others, there are dipper gourds that can be shaped into spoons, scoops, and ladles, depending on the length of the stem or "handle" which varies from 8 to 18 inches/20 to 45cm. Canteen gourds tend to be pear-shaped and are used for dishes and other vessels, up to 18 inches/45cm long. The tiniest gourds are peyote ceremonials, which were used by Central American tribes as pipes to smoke peyote, a cactus with narcotic properties, and by Amazonian tribes to carry curare for the hunt.

The quality that makes these gourds so durable and suitable for these many uses is the lignification of the rind. As the green fruit matures and dries out, it turns a natural brown color and the outer shell hardens and turns to wood. The drying-out period varies according to the water content of the gourd, but once this process is complete, the gourds should be washed in soapy water with disinfectant to kill off any fungal growth. This also helps to remove the outer skin, leaving a woody surface mottled and stained by any bacteria present when the fruit was harvested. This mottling is intrinsic to their decorative qualities.

The gourd can then simply be waxed or polished to enhance its natural colors or carved and decorated. It can be stained, painted, or engraved. A whole range of useful and decorative objects can thus be created: bowls, boxes and containers, birdhouses, lamps, dolls, and musical instruments, ranging from rattles and marimbas to string instruments and scrapers. I have even seen clocks and little cars made from gourds with a few additional parts attached.

# in the
# kitchen

*It is possible to use pumpkin or squash in the kitchen practically all year round. Summer squash and zucchini are ready for picking by mid-summer, followed by autumn squash. Then come pumpkins which are at their best in mid-October and November, from Halloween to Thanksgiving. Finally, winter squash may last until May (or even longer), taking you right through to the summer crop again. Zucchini and squash are now on sale all the time, and pumpkin is available in cans, so whether it is soups, savory dishes, vegetables, bread, pies, puddings, or pickles, pumpkins and squashes offer numerous possibilities for the creative cook.*

# Soups

Pumpkin is a versatile ingredient from which to make soup. On its own pumpkin soup is a revelation to many, but it can also serve as a rich base for a host of other ingredients. The following recipes give a broad spectrum of different combinations, but it is always exciting to experiment with new ones. Good-quality broth should be used to make the best soups. If the quantity of soup made is overwhelming, most soups freeze well.

## Cream of Pumpkin Soup

Serves 6-8

1 large onion, peeled and sliced

3½ pounds/1½kg pumpkin, peeled, seeded, and coarsely chopped

½ cup (1 stick)/125g butter

8½ cups/2 liters chicken or vegetable broth or water

salt and freshly ground black pepper

croutons, to serve (optional)

*Pumpkin soup has been made for centuries in the countries where pumpkin was a winter staple. It can be served plain, with the fine taste of the pumpkin shining through, or with modest additions of spices to give it more zest. Milk, cream, flour, and potatoes are other possible ingredients that can vary the richness and texture of the composition.*

1  In a large heavy saucepan over very low heat, melt half the butter. Add the pumpkin pieces and onion, toss to coat with the butter, and gently cook until the onion is translucent, tossing frequently.

2  Add the broth or water and season with salt and pepper to taste. Increase the heat and bring to a boil. Reduce the heat and simmer for 30 minutes, or until the pumpkin is soft.

3  Using a slotted spoon, remove the pumpkin and onion from the pot to a food processor or blender, in batches, and process until smooth. Put the purée in another pot and stir in enough of the cooking liquid until the desired consistency is reached. Taste and adjust the seasoning. (*See* page 54 for ways to vary the consistency and flavor of this soup.)

4  Add the remaining butter and reheat over low heat, stirring frequently. Sprinkle servings with some crispy croutons, if desired.

**CONSISTENCY** In this simple recipe the consistency can be altered by the addition of some milk. Indeed, a very comforting soup can be made by replacing the broth with milk and omitting the onion. Alternatively, just before serving, add a cup of light cream that has been heated through (but not allowed to boil).

To thicken the soup, make *beurre manié* by kneading ½ cup/60g of flour into the 4 tablespoons of butter reserved for adding at the end, and add this, in pieces, to the soup. Bring the soup to a boil and simmer, stirring continuously for 5 minutes, until the flour is completely cooked (test by sampling a little; uncooked flour has a "pasty" taste). The addition of 1½ pounds/750g of potatoes, which have been peeled and sliced and simmered in the soup, will give the soup body and a richer consistency.

**FLAVOR** If no onions are available or just for variety, replace them with shallots or leeks, which will do equally well. Carrots can be added to the pumpkin, with a little onion or on their own, to make an even sweeter soup. Spices can be added while the vegetables are cooking to make a more exotic-tasting soup. The possibilities are endless, but among the best are ginger (preferably grated fresh), cinnamon stick and whole cloves (both stuck in a piece of pumpkin and removed before puréeing), ground nutmeg or mace, paprika, and mild curry powder. Finally, a tablespoon or two of fresh herbs such as parsley, cilantro, chives, chervil, and tarragon can be used as a garnish.

# Pumpkin and Pasta Soup

Serves 4-6

2 pounds/1kg pumpkin, peeled, seeded, and cut into ½-inch/1-cm cubes

8 ounces/250g all-purpose potatoes, peeled and quartered

1 medium onion, peeled and thinly sliced

one 14½-ounce/400g can tomatoes or 1 pound/500g plum or large tomatoes, peeled and cut into chunks

6 cups/1½ liters vegetable broth

½ cup/125g *semi* (or rice)

½ tablespoon butter

salt and freshly ground black pepper

*Try to use* **semi de melone** *which is the tiniest of all pasta – resembling melon seeds or grains of rice. Indeed, rice, orzo (rice-shaped pasta), or vermicelli may be used as substitutes, if it is difficult to find this more unusual pasta. The* **semi** *gives the soup a smooth, thick texture and turns it into a filling, low-fat winter lunch. Serve it with chunks of whole wheat bread.*

1 Put the pumpkin, potatoes, onion, and tomatoes in a large saucepan with the broth and a big pinch each of salt and pepper. Bring to a boil over high heat. Lower the heat, cover, and cook until tender, about 20 to 30 minutes.

2 In a medium saucepan, bring some water to a boil, add salt to taste, and cook the *semi* until just *al dente* (they will swell further and absorb the vegetable flavors when added to the soup). Drain and rinse with cold water.

3 With a slotted spoon, remove the vegetables, in batches, to a food processor or blender and process until smooth. Return the purée and cooking liquid to the pan. Add the *semi* and reheat gently for a few minutes. Taste and adjust the seasoning.

4 Before serving, stir in the butter until melted.

# Cream of Pumpkin and Monkfish Soup

Serves 4-6

2 pounds/1kg pumpkin, peeled, seeded, and coarsely sliced

½ medium fennel bulb, thinly sliced

2 cups/½ liter vegetable broth or water

12 ounces/450g monkfish tails, membranes removed, cut into ¾-inch/2-cm chunks

2 cups/½ liter milk

½ tablespoon butter

salt and freshly ground black pepper

*In France, where pumpkin soup is a popular fall supper dish, fish is sometimes added to it to make a complete meal. It is important to use a fish that has a definite but not overpowering taste and a firm consistency so that it does not fall to pieces in the soup. Shrimp or scrubbed mussels will also make a scrumptious addition.*

1  Place the pumpkin and fennel (reserving some fennel fronds for garnish) in a large heavy saucepan. Add the broth or water, a big pinch each of salt and pepper, and bring to a boil over high heat. Lower the heat, cover, and cook gently for about 30 minutes until the vegetables are soft.

2  In a heavy-bottomed large saucepan, bring the milk to a simmer over medium heat. Add the monkfish, cover, and poach for about 4 minutes, turning the fish pieces once or twice, until it is just cooked. Take care not to overcook it as monkfish tends to dry out.

3  With a slotted spoon, remove the fish to a plate; cover to keep warm. Reserve the milk.

4  With a slotted spoon, remove the pumpkin and fennel to a food processor or blender, in batches, and process until smooth. Return the purée and cooking liquid to the pan, stirring in the milk in which the fish was poached. Taste and adjust the seasoning.

5  Add the fish pieces and heat thoroughly without boiling.

6  Before serving, stir in the butter and garnish with a few of the reserved fennel fronds.

# Pumpkin and Sorrel Soup

Serves 6-8

¼ cup (½ stick)/50g butter or margarine

1 large onion, peeled and finely chopped

4 medium carrots, peeled and sliced

2 pounds/1kg pumpkin, peeled, seeded, and diced

3 cups loosely packed/350g fresh sorrel leaves, stemmed and finely shredded

1 large or 2 plum tomatoes, peeled and coarsely chopped, or 8-ounce/200g can tomatoes, drained and coarsely chopped

11 cups/2½ liters vegetable or chicken broth

salt and freshly ground black pepper

*The acidity of sorrel nicely balances the sweetness of both zucchini and pumpkins. If you are unable to obtain sorrel in sufficient quantity, spinach or a mixture of both will serve as well.*

1  Melt two tablespoons of butter or margarine in a large, heavy saucepan over medium heat and sauté the onion and carrots until the onion is translucent.

2  Add the remaining vegetables to the pan with the remaining butter. Add the broth.

3  Bring to a boil over high heat. Cover, reduce the heat, and simmer for 20 minutes or so, until all the vegetables are tender. Taste and adjust the seasoning.

# Spiced Lentil and Pumpkin Soup

Serves 4-6

1 small onion, peeled and finely chopped

1 garlic clove, peeled and finely chopped

2 teaspoons grated fresh ginger

¼ cup plus 2 tablespoons/90ml vegetable oil

2 medium tomatoes, peeled and chopped

2 teaspoons mild curry powder

1 pound/500g red or yellow lentils

1 pound/500g pumpkin, peeled, seeded, and cut into 1-inch/2½-cm chunks

salt and freshly ground pepper (ideally green)

*In Nepal, the staple diet is* **dhal baat** *– lentils and rice – supplemented with vegetable curry. The following is an adaptation of* **dhal,** *to which pumpkin and liquid have been added to make a rich, nourishing soup. The ideal accompaniment would be a bowl of steamed basmati rice.*

1   In a large heavy-bottomed saucepan, over medium-high heat, heat the ¼ cup oil. Add the onion, garlic, and ginger and sauté until golden brown. Add the tomatoes.

2   Mix in the curry powder and add the lentils; reduce the heat to medium-low. Sauté for about 5 minutes, stirring frequently.

3   Add 2 cups/½ liter of water and cook until all the water is absorbed by the lentils, about 10 minutes, stirring often.

4   Stir in the pumpkin and the remaining oil. Fry for another 5 minutes, stirring frequently.

5   Add 6 cups/1½ liters of water and bring to a boil. Reduce the heat, simmer, covered, for 1 hour, until the lentils are soft. The pumpkin will be very soft and disintegrating to a purée. Taste and adjust the seasoning.

# Cream of Summer Squash and Lettuce Soup

Serves 2-4

1 pound/500g all-purpose potatoes, peeled and quartered

2 large yellow crookneck summer squash, peeled, seeded, and cut in 1-inch/2½-cm cubes

1 head lettuce, washed and coarsely chopped

1 cup/250ml milk

2 tablespoons each chopped fresh parsley, chives, and tarragon, plus more to garnish

½ cup/125ml light cream

salt and freshly ground black pepper

*This is a recipe that helped me win a "waste not, want not" battle when faced with both a large summer squash and some less than fresh lettuces. The mixture of herbs gives the soup an added complexity.*

1   Place the potatoes and squash in a large saucepan with 4½ cups/1 liter of water and a large pinch each of salt and pepper. Bring to a boil over high heat, reduce the heat, cover, and simmer for 20 minutes until the vegetables are just tender.

2   Add the chopped lettuce and milk and cook uncovered 5 minutes longer.

3   Purée the soup along with the chopped herbs, in batches, in a food processor or blender until smooth.

4   Return the soup to the saucepan and heat thoroughly. Stir in the cream and heat through, without allowing it to boil. Taste and adjust the seasoning.

5   Serve garnished with additional chopped herbs.

# Summer Squash Soup Provençale

Serves 4-6

3 tablespoons olive oil

2 medium onions, peeled and finely chopped

2 medium carrots, peeled and sliced

1 large summer squash (about 12 inches /30cm long), halved lengthwise, seeded and cut in approximately 1-inch/2½-cm cubes

one 14½-ounce/400g can tomatoes, or 1 pound/500g plum or large tomatoes, peeled and chopped

4½ cups/1liter chicken or vegetable broth

2 tablespoons chopped fresh parsley or oregano

salt and freshly ground black pepper

*One of the many ways of making use of the squash that have grown too big, this soup can be eaten either just as it is cooked or puréed to give two completely different experiences.*

1  Heat the oil over medium-low heat in a in a large heavy saucepan and add the onions and carrots. Sauté gently, until the onion becomes translucent. Add the squash and cook for a further 5 minutes, stirring frequently. Stir in the tomatoes.

2  Pour in the broth and bring to a boil. Reduce the heat and simmer for 20 minutes, until the carrots are cooked and the squash tender. Taste and adjust the seasoning.

3  Serve as it is, with a garnish of parsley or oregano. Alternatively, purée in a food processor or blender and reheat if necessary. Garnish as above.

# Cream of Zucchini Soup with Blue Cheese

Serves 4-6

2 pounds/1kg zucchini

2 tablespoons/25g margarine

2 tablespoons/25g all-purpose flour

2 cups/½ liter chicken or vegetable broth

½ cup/125ml light cream

2 ounces/50g mild creamy blue cheese (Saga blue is delicious), rind removed and diced

salt and freshly ground black pepper

*In the 1890 edition of her* **Book of Household Management,** *Isabella Beeton gives a recipe for vegetable marrow soup: young vegetable marrows (zucchini to us), cream, broth, salt, and pepper. Here is a more sophisticated version using a* **roux** *to thicken the soup.*

1  Wash the zucchini, then peel two of them with a stripper to make thin strips. Refrigerate the strips in a plastic bag for garnishing the soup later.

2  Slice all the zucchini. Place in a large skillet with 2 cups/½ liter of water. Bring to a boil, simmer, covered, until quite tender.

3  Meanwhile make a *roux*: Melt the margarine in a heavy-bottomed saucepan over medium heat, add the flour, stir to blend fully, and cook for a minute, stirring constantly. Gradually whisk in the broth to make a white sauce, adding small quantities at first and making sure that they are thoroughly absorbed before adding any more.

4  Bring the white sauce to a boil and simmer for 5 minutes, to ensure that the flour is thoroughly cooked. Stir constantly to avoid any lumps forming.

5  When the zucchini are cooked, place them in a food processor or blender with their cooking liquid and process until smooth.

6  Transfer the zucchini purée to the saucepan and blend in the white sauce. Add the cream. Heat through carefully without allowing to boil. Taste and adjust the seasoning.

7  Serve garnished with the diced blue cheese and the reserved strips of zucchini peel.

# Savories

Pumpkins and squashes will happily associate with a variety of other foods to make the most delicious savories. The combinations are almost endless and the results can vary from delectable cocktail nibbles to hearty one-dish meals. In many cases, most varieties of winter squash can be used in place of pumpkin. Some of the recipes in this section are simple and quick to make, others require more preparation but are well worth the effort, particularly if you are entertaining friends.

## Little Zucchini, Tomato and Basil Biscuits

Makes about 38

2 cups/250g self-rising flour

⅓ cup/75g cold margarine, cut into bits

1 small zucchini, finely grated (½ cup/80g)

2 tablespoons sun-dried tomato bits (not packed in oil)

1 teaspoon prepared pesto

⅓ cup/80ml buttermilk

*These biscuits are among the best goodies to offer at a summer cocktail party. They are light, melt in the mouth, and will disappear fast, so make enough for two or three per person. You can also split them and spread with cream cheese or serve them with soup.*

1  Heat the oven to 450°F/230°C. Grease two baking sheets.

2  Place the flour in a large bowl. Cut in the margarine until the mixture looks like corn meal.

3  With a fork or with your hands, mix in the zucchini and sun-dried tomato bits.

4  Stir the pesto into the buttermilk and add all at once to the flour mixture. Combine just until the dough is blended. (Dough will be a bit crumbly.)

5  Turn out onto a lightly floured surface, dip you hands in flour, and knead the dough lightly and briefly for no more than 30 seconds.

6  Pat or roll the dough to a ⅛-inch/½-cm thickness. Cut out the biscuits with a floured 1½-inch/3½-cm round cutter. Re-roll and cut scraps once.

7  Place on the prepared baking sheets, spaced apart. Bake for 7–10 minutes, until an even light brown. Transfer to wire racks and cool to warm. Served freshly baked.

# Little Zucchini Tarts

Serves 4

1½ pounds/750g small zucchini, thinly sliced

2 tablespoons salt

½ recipe for rich shortcrust pastry, chilled (*see* Pumpkin Meringue Pie, page 91)

1 tablespoon extra virgin olive oil

1 tablespoon prepared pesto

1 tablespoon plain yogurt

*These little zucchini tarts are very simple to make and are an easy alternative to quiche. They are always a great success, particularly appreciated by friends who prefer not to eat eggs. I have also tried them with red pesto, a mix that includes basil, sun-dried tomatoes, and pine nuts.*

1  Place the zucchini slices in a colander and toss with the salt. Let drain for 30 minutes or so.
2  Preheat the oven to 400°F/200°C. Line 4 individual tartlet pans which measure about 4½ inches/11cm across with the pastry. Place tartlet pans on baking sheets. Cover with circles of wax paper, weight with beans, and bake blind for 15–20 minutes, until just beginning to color. Remove to a wire rack to cool.
3  Rinse the zucchini to remove excess salt and dry well with a clean cloth or paper towel.
4  Heat the oil in a large skillet and sauté the zucchini briskly over high heat until golden brown, stirring frequently to prevent them from burning.
5  Mix the pesto and yogurt with the zucchini and divide this equally between the pre-baked pastry shells. Place on baking sheets.
6  Bake for 10–15 minutes, until the tarts are heated through and the pastry is cooked. Serve immediately.

# Pumpkin Quiche

Serves 6

1 pound/500g rich shortcrust pastry, chilled (*see* Pumpkin Meringue Pie, page 91)

1 medium onion, peeled and chopped

2 tablespoons/30g butter

3 eggs, separated

½ cup/125ml light cream

1 pound/500g pumpkin, cooked and mashed (1 cup mashed)

3 tablespoons finely diced ham

1 tablespoon chopped fresh parsley

salt and freshly ground black pepper

*Quiches are popular standbys for light meals or parties. They can be made in advance and eaten cold or reheated. In the following recipes both zucchini and pumpkins are pressed into service — the zucchini slices remain intact within the egg mixture, while the pumpkin is mashed and incorporated into it.*

1  Preheat the oven to 350°F/180°C. Roll out the pastry and use it to line a 9-inch/23-cm quiche pan with 2-inch/5-cm sides.
2  In a small skillet, sauté the onion in the butter until translucent.
3  In a large bowl, whisk the egg yolks lightly and combine with the cream. Whisk in the pumpkin, ham, onion, and parsley. Season with a generous pinch each of salt and pepper.
4  With an electric mixer at high speed, beat the egg whites until stiff and fold into the pumpkin mixture. Place the quiche pan on a baking sheet. Pour the mixture into the pastry shell and bake for 30–35 minutes, or until nicely puffed up and set. Transfer to a wire rack.
5  Serve hot, cold, or gently reheated – it is even better the next day! Refrigerate leftovers.

# Zucchini Quiche

Serves 6

1 pound/500g rich shortcrust pastry, chilled (*see* Pumpkin Meringue Pie, page 91)

2 tablespoons/30g butter

3 shallots, thinly sliced

4 slices of bacon, cut into ½-inch/1-cm squares

1 pound/500g zucchini, thinly sliced

1 teaspoon chopped fresh savory or sage

½ cup/125ml cottage cheese

2 egg yolks, plus 1 whole egg

2 tablespoons grated Cheddar or any other tasty hard cheese

3 tablespoons soft fresh whole wheat bread crumbs

salt and freshly ground black pepper

1 Preheat the oven to 400°F/200°C. Roll out the pastry to about ¼-inch/½-cm thickness and use it to line a shallow 9-inch/23-cm loose-bottomed tart pan. Chill again for 30 minutes. Line the pastry shell with a piece of wax paper or foil, weight with some beans, and bake blind for 15 minutes, until it begins to color at the edges. Remove from the oven to a wire rack. Keep the oven at the same setting.

2 Melt the butter in a large skillet over medium heat. Add the shallots, then the bacon and finally the zucchini. Gently sauté, turning occasionally, until the zucchini just begins to color. Stir in the savory or sage.

3 Meanwhile, in a medium bowl, beat together the cottage cheese, egg yolks and whole egg. Season with a little salt (remember that the bacon and cheese are salted) and some black pepper.

4 Place the tart pan on a baking sheet. Spoon the zucchini mixture into the pastry shell and pour the egg mixture over the top. Mix together the grated cheese and bread crumbs and scatter over the top of the quiche.

5 Bake for 20–25 minutes, or until the egg mixture is set and the topping is golden brown. Transfer to a wire rack to cool briefly.

6 Serve warm or cold. Refrigerate leftovers.

# Zucchini with Chicken and Yogurt

Serves 2-3

1 pound/500g zucchini, cut into ½-inch/1-cm slices

1 tablespoon olive oil

1 tablespoon chopped fresh rosemary

2 cooked chicken breast halves, skinned and cut into strips

3 tablespoons plain yogurt

salt and freshly ground black pepper

*I first devised this dish to offer a change from the usual onion, tomato, and chicken casserole I made to use up the leftovers of the weekend bird. It is delicious, and so quick and easy to make that I frequently buy some roast chicken pieces to make it for a midweek supper for two or three. Serve with rice or new potatoes.*

1 Blanch the zucchini slices in a pot of boiling salted water for 3–5 minutes until just crisp-tender. Drain and blot dry with a clean tea towel or paper towels.

2 Heat the oil in a large skillet over medium heat and sauté the zucchini for 5 minutes, stirring frequently.

3 Add the rosemary, chicken, a large pinch each of salt and pepper, and finally the yogurt. Cook briskly, tossing frequently, for another couple of minutes until heated through and the flavors are blended.

4 Serve immediately.

# Pollack with Zucchini

Serves 4

1 tablespoon vegetable oil

1 pound/500g zucchini, thinly sliced lengthwise

about 1½ pounds/750g pollack fillets, cut into 4 portions

8 ounces/250g ripe tomatoes, quartered

2 teaspoons chopped fresh basil or marjoram

1 garlic clove, peeled and chopped or crushed

juice of ½ lemon

salt and freshly ground black pepper

*The following recipe is taken from* **The Friends of the Earth Cookbook** *and is reproduced with kind permission from its author, Veronica Sekules.*

*Many white fish tend to be a little dry when cooked on their own and require moist accompaniments. Both the zucchini and the tomatoes contribute plenty of moisture to the dish. Cooked in this manner, the zucchini retain a crunchy texture that contrasts with that of the baked fish. In addition, the delicate flavor of the zucchini complements this mild-flavored fish. This recipe is also suitable for scrod, cod, backfish, or grouper.*

1 Preheat the oven to 350°F/180°C.
2 Rub a little of the oil around a shallow 9x13-inch/23x39-cm ovenproof dish. Lay a few of the zucchini slices in the dish and then place the fish fillets on top. Arrange the rest of the zucchini and the tomatoes over them. Sprinkle with the herbs, garlic, lemon juice, salt and pepper to taste, and the remaining oil.
3 Cover with oiled parchment paper or foil and bake for half an hour, or until the fish is cooked.

# Mexican-style Pumpkin and Bean Stew

Serves 4-6

¼ cup/50g bacon fat or vegetable oil

1 large onion, peeled and coarsely chopped

2 pounds/1kg pumpkin, peeled, seeded, and coarsely cubed

2 large red bell peppers, seeded and sliced

one 15-ounce/425g can of red kidney beans, rinsed and drained

one 15-ounce/425g can of black-eyed peas, rinsed and drained

2 large or 4 plum tomatoes, peeled and coarsely chopped, or one 14½-ounce/400g can of chopped tomatoes

4 mild chilies, parboiled, tops removed, and chopped or one 4-ounce/125g can diced green chilies

3 garlic cloves, peeled and finely chopped

salt and freshly ground black pepper

*This recipe produces a zesty and warming, nutritious dish that is delicious served with chunks of homemade whole-grain bread or tortillas.*

1 In a large heavy-bottomed saucepan, heat the bacon fat or vegetable oil over medium–low heat. Add the onion and sauté until translucent.
2 Add the pumpkin and toss to coat the pieces in fat. Cook for 5 minutes, stirring often. Stir in the bell peppers and cook for 5 minutes more.
3 Stir in the remaining ingredients and bring to a boil over medium heat. Reduce the heat, cover, and simmer for 20–30 minutes, or until the pumpkin is just soft. Taste and season with salt and pepper.

# Zucchini and Wild Rice

Serves 4

4 ounces/125g wild rice, washed and drained

one 14½-ounce/425g can of tomatoes

2 cups/½ liter of duck or vegetable broth

2 tablespoons butter

1 medium onion, peeled and finely chopped

4 ounces/125g lean slab bacon, in one piece, or 4 thick slices, cut into cubes

1 pound/500g zucchini, halved lengthwise and cut into thick crosswise slices

*Wild rice is, in fact, the seed from an aquatic grass that grows on the lake shores of northern Minnesota and southern Ontario. It has a stronger, nuttier flavor and a more robust consistency than rice. It is always a treat.*

1 Put the rice, tomatoes, and broth in a medium ovenproof casserole. Bring to a boil over high heat, cover, reduce the heat, and simmer for 30 minutes.

2 Meanwhile, melt the butter in a large skillet and fry the onion and bacon for 5–10 minutes, stirring frequently, until the onion is translucent.

3 Add the zucchini and continue cooking for another 10-15 minutes or until lightly browned. Remove from the heat.

4 When the rice has been cooking for 30 minutes, check to see if it is nearly cooked – each grain should be splitting and showing white beneath the black husk. When it has reached this stage, add the zucchini mixture and cook for an additional 15 minutes, so that all the flavors mingle. If a little more liquid is required, swish it around the skillet to collect the pan juices before adding to the rice and tomatoes.

# Pumpkin Risotto

Serves 6

4½ cups/1 liter vegetable or chicken broth

3 tablespoons olive oil

¼ cup (½ stick)/50g butter

1 medium onion, peeled and thinly sliced

1 sprig of fresh thyme

1 bay leaf

1 pound/500g pumpkin, peeled, seeded and cut into ½-inch/1-cm cubes

1½ cups/330g risotto rice, such as Arborio

½ cup/125ml dry white wine

3 tablespoons grated Parmesan cheese

12 black olives, pitted and halved

salt and freshly ground black pepper

*Pumpkin risotto comes in two versions. Cooked and puréed pumpkin can be added to cooked rice or, as is done here, pumpkin pieces can be cooked with the rice.*

1 Bring the broth to a boil in a medium saucepan.

2 In a large heavy-bottomed skillet, heat the oil and 1 tablespoon of butter and sauté the onion until golden. Add a ladleful of hot broth, the thyme, and bay leaf. Stir for a few minutes until almost absorbed.

3 Add the pumpkin pieces and toss to coat. Cover and cook for 10 minutes, turning the pumpkin occasionally. Add more broth as the pan gets dry.

4 Stir in the rice and cook until it begins to turn translucent. Add the wine and stir until well absorbed.

5 Add more broth, a ladleful at a time, stirring slowly until the rice has absorbed the previous addition but never letting it dry out.

6 About 15 minutes after adding the rice, or a few minutes before it is quite tender, remove from the heat. Add the rest of the butter, the cheese, and the olives. Stir gently, being careful to keep the rice moist. Taste and season with salt and pepper.

7 Replace the lid and let the risotto rest for 3–4 minutes, until the rice is soft and creamy. Serve immediately.

# Winter Squash Rissoles

Serves 4

8 ounces/250g cooked ground beef
1 medium onion, peeled and minced
1 teaspoon horseradish sauce
1 cup/250ml cold winter squash purée
⅔ cup/90g whole wheat bread crumbs
2 eggs, beaten
oatmeal or cornmeal for coating
vegetable oil for shallow frying
salt and freshly ground black pepper

*This recipe is an Australian idea in which the winter squash makes leftover meat go a little further (or perhaps the meat makes leftover mashed squash go further?). Choose a variety with solid flesh, such as a butternut or hubbard. If you don't have leftover squash, use a package of frozen puréed squash. Serve with french fries and a crisp mixed salad.*

1 In a large mixing bowl, thoroughly combine the beef, onion, horseradish sauce, squash, and bread crumbs. Add a big pinch each of salt and pepper. Cover and let rest in the refrigerator for about 30 minutes.

2 Form the chilled mixture into 8 firm patties, about 1-inch/2½-cm thick. Coat them in the beaten egg and dredge in a little oatmeal or cornmeal.

3 In a large heavy, non-stick skillet, heat some oil over medium heat. Add the patties and fry for 5 minutes on each side, until the coating is crisp and golden and the inside piping hot.

# Potato and Winter Squash Pie

Serves 6

1 pound/500g flaky pastry, chilled
(*see* Pumpkin Pie page 90)

butter for pie pan
2 pounds/1kg potatoes, peeled and thinly sliced
2 medium onions, peeled and chopped
1 pound/500g butternut squash, peeled, seeded, and thinly sliced
⅔ cup/165ml heavy cream
beaten egg or milk to glaze
salt and freshly ground black pepper

*Potato pie has many regional variations in France. My uncle, from the north of the country, used to make one from flaky pastry with the cream added before cooking. In the Bourbonnais (central France) it is made with puff pastry and the cream is poured through the top funnel when it is cooked. The following recipe also contains winter squash – a dry-fleshed variety, such as butternut or hubbard, is best – and looks stunning when cut.*

1 Preheat the oven to 400°F/200°C. Butter a 9-inch/23-cm deep-dish pie pan. Roll out two-thirds of the pastry to about ¼-inch/½-cm thickness and use it to line the prepared pie pan, leaving plenty of overlap at the edge.

2 Put a layer of potato slices in the pastry case, followed by a little onion. Season with salt and pepper. Top with a layer of squash slices and a little more onion and season. Repeat layers until you have used all the vegetables. Carefully pour over the cream. Fold the pastry edges up around the vegetables and glaze the outside.

3 Roll out the remaining pastry to an 8-inch/20-cm circle. Trim a bit for decorating. Cover the pie with the pastry, overlapping and sealing the edges carefully. Decorate with pastry scraps. Make a vent for the steam or prick over with a fork and glaze with egg or a little milk.

4 Place pie on a baking sheet. Bake for 1 hour, or until the pastry is golden and the filling is cooked. (Test the vegetables by sticking a skewer through them.) If the pastry is coloring too much before the vegetables are cooked , lower the temperature to 350°F/180°C.

# Tortelli di Mantova

for the filling:

1¼ pounds/600g pumpkin, peeled, seeded, and cut into ½-inch/1-cm pieces

2 eggs

salt

freshly grated nutmeg to taste

3½ ounces/100g *mostarda* (apple slices), finely chopped

½ cup/60g fine plain dry bread crumbs

1⅛ pounds/500g Parmesan cheese, grated

3½ ounces/100g amaretti cookies (14 half cookies or 7 wrapped, 2 in each wrapper), finely crushed (first removing bits of sugar on top)

a little warm milk, if necessary

for the pasta:

3½ cups/400g all-purpose flour or combination of 1¾ cups/200g all-purpose flour and 1¾ cups/200g whole wheat flour

4 eggs

alternatively, use 14 ounces/400g prepared fresh pasta dough

salt for cooking

for the sage butter dressing:

¾ cup (1½ sticks)/200g butter

2-3 sage leaves

*Tortelli are little pasta parcels filled with pumpkin. This recipe was given to me by Anna-Maria Fiozzi, a Mantuan friend and excellent cook in the traditional Italian style.* **Mostarda** *is candied fruit preserved in mustard-flavored syrup. For this recipe, the fruit should be preferably apples, but this may be difficult to find. The addition of* **mostarda** *is important but you may substitute ⅓ cup finely chopped apple mixed with half a teaspoon of Dijon mustard.*

1  Make the filling: Steam the pumpkin until just tender. While still warm, mash it with a fork in a large bowl, then let it cool completely.

2  Add the eggs, a pinch of salt and grated nutmeg, the chopped *mostarda* (or apple and mustard), the bread crumbs, 4 cups/400g of the Parmesan, and the crumbled amaretti. Mix thoroughly; the consistency should be quite firm, but if it is too dense, add a little warm milk.

3  Make the pasta: Sift the flour into a mound on a work surface. Break the eggs into a well in the middle of the mounded flour. Beat the eggs with a fork and gradually work in the flour, until it is all combined. Knead the dough until smooth and satiny and shape it into a ball. Cover the dough with a dry towel and let the dough rest for 30 minutes in a cool place.

4  Roll out the dough on a floured board with a rolling pin (in as large quantities as you can manage) until very thin. Successful tortelli requires the dough to be as thin as possible.

5  Using a large crinkle-edged pastry wheel, cut into strips 4 inches/10cm wide.

6  Make the tortelli: Put a rounded teaspoon of filling at 1¼-inch/3-cm intervals on the dough, to one side of the strip and fold the strip over down the middle. Run the pastry wheel down the folded side. Press down the dough with your fingers around the filling. Run the pastry cutter between the filling mounds to make individual tortelli. They should be about 2¼-inches/6-cm square. Be sure the dough encloses the filling. Put the tortelli on a tray lined with some wax paper or a tea towel.

7  Bring a large pot of water to a boil.

8  Make the dressing: Melt the butter in a small heavy-bottomed saucepan and add the sage leaves. Leave to infuse over a low heat — the butter should turn golden but take care not to burn it. Remove from the heat and cover to keep warm.

9  When the water is boiling, add a rounded tablespoon of salt and drop in the tortelli while maintaining a good rolling boil. When they rise to the top, remove them with a slotted spoon and layer them in a large warm dish with the melted sage butter dressing and remaining Parmesan cheese (tortelli, dressing, and Parmesan, then repeat).

10  Serve the tortelli warm. If some are left over, you can eat them the day after warmed through in the oven. This is very nice, as they form a crust.

# Spiralli with Zucchini

Serves 2-3

2 tablespoons olive oil

3 shallots, thinly sliced

1 pound/500g zucchini, thinly sliced

2 teaspoons chopped fresh thyme

½ cup/40g (about 18 halves) sun-dried tomatoes, soaked for 20 minutes in hot water and drained

1 tablespoon salt

freshly ground black pepper

8 ounces/225g spiralli (or any other short pasta, such as fusilli or penne)

2 tablespoons freshly grated Parmesan cheese, to serve

*There are numerous ways of preparing zucchini to accompany pasta. The following recipe makes a simple yet tasty meal when served with a crunchy green salad.*

1 Heat the olive oil in a large skillet over medium-low heat. Gently sauté the shallots and zucchini until they begin to brown. Season with a big pinch each of salt and pepper, then add the thyme and tomatoes. Heat through, remove from the heat, cover, and keep warm.

2 Bring to a boil a large saucepan of water. Add the 1 tablespoon of salt and then the pasta. Rapidly bring back to a boil and cook at a rolling boil until the pasta is *al dente*.

3 Drain the pasta and return it to the pan. Top with the zucchini mixture.

4 Serve immediately with Parmesan sprinkled over the top.

# Zucchini Lasagne

Serves 4-6

3 medium zucchini

2 tablespoons olive oil

2 medium onions, peeled and coarsely chopped

1 garlic clove, peeled and minced

6 large mushrooms, chopped

1 tablespoon chopped fresh thyme

one 14½-ounce/400g can of chopped tomatoes

1 tablespoon chopped fresh basil

salt

8 ounces/250g mozzarella cheese, shredded

1 pound/500g ricotta or cottage cheese (or a mixture of the two)

12 sheets no-boil lasagne noodles

3 tablespoons freshly grated Parmesan cheese

freshly ground black pepper

*The combination of zucchini and mushrooms makes a tasty filling for this vegetarian lasagne. The tomatoes are included separately to distinguish the flavors, but all three ingredients contribute moisture that is soaked up by the cooking pasta. There is no need for béchamel or white sauce in this recipe; just mix the cheeses together and spread them over the top.*

1 Preheat the oven to 350°F/180°C. Grate two of the zucchini and thinly slice the third.

2 Over medium heat, in a large skillet, heat 1 tablespoon of the olive oil and sauté half the onion with the garlic, mushrooms, grated zucchini, and thyme for about 10 minutes, stirring frequently.

3 In a separate skillet, sauté the rest of the onion in the remaining oil until tender. Add the tomatoes and basil and bring to a boil. Reduce the heat, season with salt, and simmer for a further 10 minutes until slightly thickened.

4 Mix together the mozzarella and ricotta or cottage cheese in a blender.

5 Put half the tomato sauce in the bottom of a 11x7-inch/27x17-cm baking pan and cover with two sheets of pasta. Follow with half the zucchini mixture, then two sheets of pasta, topped with half the cheese mixture. Repeat layering and then top with the sliced zucchini.

6 Sprinkle with Parmesan and bake for 40 minutes or until hot and bubbly. Serve with freshly ground pepper.

# Stuffed Pumpkin

1 medium pumpkin or winter squash

2 tablespoons vegetable oil

2 medium onions, peeled and chopped

2 medium carrots, peeled and sliced

1 large red bell pepper, seeded and chopped

1 celery stalk, chopped

1 large tomato or 2 plum tomatoes, seeded, peeled, and chopped

one 15-ounce/425g can of lima beans, rinsed and drained

salt and freshly ground black pepper

1 cup plus 2 tablespoons/120g whole wheat bread crumbs

for the cheese sauce:

2 tablespoons/30g butter

2 tablespoons/30g all-purpose flour

1 cup/250ml milk

3½ ounces (1 cup)/100g grated Cheddar cheese (or any other tasty hard cheese)

*Pumpkins and squashes are ideal containers for stuffing. Their water content ensures that the stuffing remains moist and imparts all its flavor to the pumpkin as the whole thing bakes in the oven. There is an infinite variety of combinations to choose from for the stuffing. This recipe is for a vegetarian stuffing with lima beans as the main protein ingredient. It is topped with a cheese sauce that gives the dish additional richness. Bring the dish to the table in a whole pumpkin or in several smaller pumpkins, each serving one or two people.*

1 Preheat the oven to 325°F/170°C.

2 Prepare the pumpkin by cutting a lid and scooping out the pith and seeds with a metal spoon. Slice a little cut from the bottom so that the pumpkin stands upright.

3 Over medium heat, in a large saucepan, heat the oil and sauté the onions until translucent. Add the carrots, bell pepper, celery, and tomatoes. Cook for 10 minutes. Stir in the lima beans. Season to taste with salt and pepper and remove from the heat.

4 Make the cheese sauce: Melt the butter in a medium heavy-bottomed saucepan and stir in the flour until blended. Slowly add the milk, whisking well after each addition. Simmer for 5 minutes, stirring constantly, until the flour is cooked and the sauce thick. Remove from the heat, whisk in the cheese, taste, and adjust the seasoning.

5 Place the pumpkin in a large roasting pan. Carefully spoon the vegetables into the pumpkin, cover with the bread crumbs, and pour the cheese sauce on top. Replace the lid and bake in the oven for 1 hour, until the pumpkin is soft but not falling apart.

6 Serve by scooping out the filling and sauce, together with some pumpkin from the sides.

# Stuffed Zucchini

6 Ronde de Nice zucchini or
12 medium zucchini

for the tomato sauce:

1 tablespoon olive oil

1 medium onion, peeled and finely chopped

1 carrot, peeled and chopped

3 large tomatoes or 6 plum tomatoes, peeled
and coarsely chopped

1 tablespoon chopped fresh parsley

1 tablespoon chopped fresh basil

salt and freshly ground black pepper

for the stuffing:

3 tablespoons precooked couscous, soaked in
3 tablespoons boiling water

1 egg, lightly beaten

2 medium onions, peeled and finely chopped

8 ounces/250g ground lamb

1 tablespoon chopped fresh cilantro

2 tablespoons chopped fresh thyme
(or 1 tablespoon dried)

1 tablespoon chopped fresh mint
(or 1½ teaspoons dried)

salt and freshly ground black pepper

*The meaty stuffing for this recipe has a North African influence and includes couscous, a staple made from durum wheat semolina, lamb, cilantro, thyme, and mint. Ronde de Nice zucchini are an heirloom variety of squash, producing a round light green zucchini.*

1  Preheat the oven to 350°F/180°C.

2  If using Ronde de Nice zucchini, cut a thin slice from the end of each so that they stand upright in a dish. If you are using conventional zucchini, trim the ends. Boil them whole for 5–10 minutes, depending on how large they are, until just tender. Drain and let cool.

3  Make the tomato sauce: In a medium heavy-bottomed saucepan, heat the oil over medium heat and sauté the onion until translucent. Add the carrot, tomatoes, and herbs. Season lightly with salt and pepper; bring to a boil. Reduce the heat, cover, and simmer gently for 20 minutes. Either press the sauce through a fine-mesh strainer or purée in a food processor.

4  Make the stuffing by thoroughly mixing all the ingredients in a bowl with a big pinch each of salt and pepper.

5  When the zucchini are cool enough to handle, cut a lid either from the top of the Ronde de Nice squash or the side of the regular zucchini. Scoop out seeds from squash with a teaspoon, making a cavity. (Try using an apple corer for long zucchini.) Fill the cavities with stuffing. Replace the lids.

6  Place the stuffed zucchini in an ovenproof dish that has a tight-fitting lid. Pour in the tomato sauce, cover, and bake for 20 minutes or until the stuffing is heated through and the sauce is bubbly.

# Vegetable Dishes

Pumpkins and winter squashes are delicious as a vegetable and, from harvest until early spring, I look forward to bringing a good-sized pumpkin or winter squash into the kitchen. Over the years I have developed a routine to cope with the sheer volume of fruit and I find that it is no longer the daunting task it was in the early days. From each fruit I like to make a soup and one savory dish; I may make a cake or sweet dish. I will also have pumpkin as a vegetable for several days, in the same way that we eat potatoes with most meals. And I always freeze some as purée for later use.

The simplest way of preparing pumpkin or winter squash is steaming or roasting it and serving it with a pat of butter and brown sugar or a sprinkling of parsley. They are equally delicious served with a mushroom, tomato, or cheese sauce. Here are a few other ideas – most are easy to do, and the results are always colorful on the plate.

## Vegetable Spaghetti

Spaghetti squash is an oddity that deserves to be better known and more frequently used. It is light and fresh to eat and, provided the accompanying sauce is low-fat, manna to a weight-watcher.

Spaghetti squash can either be plunged into a large saucepan of boiling water or baked in a moderate oven (350°F/180°C) for about an hour or until the skin begins to break. Before baking, remember to puncture the skin several times to allow steam to escape, thus preventing explosions and nasty messes. In both cases the squash is cooked when it is easily pierced with a sharp knife.

Hold the cooked squash with a towel or oven mitts, cut it across the middle. Then remove the seeds and pith with a spoon, and, using a fork, pull the flesh away from the sides. It will come away in long strands that look just like spaghetti.

It is most delicious eaten plain as a vegetable side dish with a good chunk of butter, salt, and freshly ground pepper, but can also be served au gratin with grated Cheddar, Gruyère, or other hard cheese. Alternatively, you can use it as a substitute for pasta, and serve it with a variety of sauces.

# Pumpkins and Winter Squashes

**PREPARATION**   Unless you are stuffing the pumpkin or using it as a vessel for soup, the first task is to cut a manageable piece from the fruit. Use a large sharp knife for this, then remove the seeds and stringy flesh with a spoon. Cut the segment into wedges approximately 1 inch/2½ cm wide and remove the skin. The pumpkin is now ready for use, whether in whole pieces or for puréeing.

**STEAMING AND STEWING**   The pumpkin pieces can be steamed for 10–20 minutes until tender. Alternatively, they may be stewed in a covered saucepan on low heat. You will initially need to add a little water to prevent the pieces from sticking to the pan and scorching, but then the fruit releases plenty of moisture in which to cook. This method will take 20–30 minutes for the flesh to be tender.

**ROASTING INDIVIDUAL PUMPKINS AND WINTER SQUASHES**   You can successfully roast whole all the smaller varieties of pumpkins and winter squashes including the tiniest, such as Jack-be-Little and Rolet. Puncture with a skewer to let the steam escape. Slightly larger ones, such as the butternut and acorn squashes, should be cut in half before baking. A good tip: Microwave the squash for 1–2 minutes, place it on a towel to keep it steady, then halve or quarter it. Roast squash are delicious just as they are, with a little butter or a bit of spice — consider one or two teaspoons of ginger, nutmeg, or cinnamon, and some sugar. Bake at 350°F/180°C for between 45 minutes to 1 hour until tender when pierced with a fork.

You may roast a whole or half pumpkin (place this cut-side down in a lightly oiled roasting pan) and then cut and seed it. The skin will become much softer during cooking. Alternatively, pumpkin or hubbard squash may be roasted in wedges, with the washed skin still attached. As a rough guide, you will need about 8 ounces/250g pumpkin per person.

**MAKING A PURÉE**   Cook the pumpkin by one of the methods described above until the flesh is very tender. It can then be mashed easily with a fork or put it through a food mill or food processor (you may need to add a bit of liquid). You now have the basic ingredient for many recipes that use pumpkin, and it is simple to freeze any quantity. For use in recipes, freeze in 1-cup amounts in labelled freezer bags or containers. If making quiches, pies, bread, or cakes, winter squash purée is sometimes better to use than that of the large, orange-skinned pumpkin as it tends to be drier. If the purée is watery, simmer it over low heat in a heavy-bottomed pan rather than draining off the liquid as this removes much of the goodness of the fruit. Growing conditions will affect the nature of the fruit and the purée. A cool, rainy season will produce extremely moist and stringy flesh; conversely, hot, dry weather will produce dry fruit. Canned pumpkin purée or frozen puréed squash is a useful substitute and will work in any of the recipes calling for fresh pumpkin or squash purée.

# Summer Squash

**BOILING** One of my favorite summer vegetable dishes is a bowl of tiny zucchini and summer squash that have been cooked whole in a large pan of boiling water for a few minutes (5–10, depending on their sizes), drained, and served with plenty of butter, some sea salt, and freshly ground black pepper. All the colors and shapes are a great attraction and are frequently the topic of conversation for the few minutes following their arrival at the table.

**FRYING** More frequently, zucchini and summer squash are fried or sauted, either in olive oil or butter. If they are over 6 inches/15cm long, you may wish to slice the squash, toss with salt in a colander (1 tablespoon of salt for 2 pounds/1kg zucchini) and let drain for about an hour. They will then release water and as a result, absorb much less fat when cooking. Rinse, drain, and pat them dry with a cloth or paper towel before cooking them.

A variety of herbs that associate particularly well with zucchini can be added to the skillet while sautéing. The best to my mind are rosemary and sweet basil, followed closely by thyme, parsley, and cilantro. Do not try to mix them.

For a somewhat richer dish, add ⅔ cup/165ml of gently heated and seasoned light cream and some slivered almonds or pine nuts. Tiny shallots, silver-skinned onions, or scallions also make good accompaniments to zucchini. The secret is not to add too many or they will overpower the flavor of the squash.

Squash can also be fried in batter. The best way of doing this is to slice pieces diagonally and then soak them in some milk for 10 minutes or so. Coat them in flour and then deep-fry at a very high temperature. This ensures that the coating is cooked, and the squash hot but still wonderfully crunchy.

# Pumpkin and Squash Gratins and Cheese Bakes

*Pumpkins and squashes are perfect ingredients for making rich cheesy gratins. One of my favorite recipes is very simple to make.*

Sauté slices of skinned winter squash in some butter in a skillet until tender and pile in an ovenproof dish in alternate layers with sliced onion that has been cooked gently in some butter until transluscent. Top with a layer of grated hard cheese such as Gruyère or Emmentaler for a stringy effect, or Cheddar for a crisper finish (it often depends on what is in the fridge — and may be a mixture), combined with some fresh bread crumbs (white or whole wheat) or pumpkin seeds, which give a good crunchy texture. Bake at 350°F/180°C for 15–20 minutes until the topping is golden brown and crunchy.

Other recipes include tomatoes, or, as in the following one, zucchini, potatoes, and onions. If you are making a gratin or bake in advance or want to freeze it, prepare up to the point of baking. If frozen, it will need to be defrosted for approximately three hours at room temperature or 45 minutes in the oven at 300°F/150°C, then raise the temperature to 350°F/180°C, for 15 minutes to crisp the topping.

# Zucchini, Potato, and Onion Bake

Serves 2-3

butter for the dish
2 medium white onions
2 medium potatoes
3 medium zucchini
5 ounces/150g Gruyère or Emmentaler cheese, thinly sliced

1  Preheat the oven to 425°F/220°C and lightly butter an 8-inch/20-cm square baking pan.
2  In as little water as possible, boil together the onions, potatoes, and zucchini in a large saucepan. Remove the zucchini as soon as they are cooked. (Reserve about 3 tablespoons of the cooking liquid.)
3  Slice the cooked vegetables while they are still hot and put them in layers in the prepared dish, starting with the zucchini, followed by the onions and finally the potatoes. Add the reserved cooking liquid. Cover the potatoes with the cheese slices.
4  Bake for 10 minutes or until the cheese is melted and bubbly.

# Ratatouille

Serves 4-6

3 tablespoons olive oil

1 large onion, peeled and sliced

1 medium eggplant, sliced

1 large red bell pepper, seeded and cut into strips

4 medium zucchini, sliced

4 large tomatoes, peeled and quartered

1 or 2 garlic cloves, peeled and finely chopped (optional)

2 tablespoons chopped fresh parsley

1 tablespoon chopped fresh thyme

2 bay leaves

salt and freshly ground black pepper

1 In a deep heavy-bottomed saucepan, heat the oil over medium–low heat and add the onion. Cook gently until tender and translucent but not golden.

2 Add the eggplant and pepper, and turn them to ensure that they are coated in oil. Sauté for 2 to 3 minutes.

3 Add the zucchini, then the tomatoes, garlic (if using), and herbs. Give the mixture a careful stir and heat thoroughly.

4 Simmer uncovered for 40–50 minutes, turning occasionally, until the vegetables are soft but not disintegrating — the liquid should be well reduced by now. Taste and season with a pinch each of salt and pepper.

5 Serve hot or cold. Any leftovers can be warmed up again; ratatouille tastes even better the second time around.

# Pumpkin Shoots

Serves 4

16 soft tips from pumpkin shoots (top 4 inches/10cm)

¼ cup/60ml vegetable oil

4 garlic cloves, peeled and finely chopped

1 large onion, peeled and chopped

1 teaspoon salt

1 teaspoon ground cardamom

2 teaspoons mild curry powder

¼ cup/10g chopped cilantro

1 medium green or sweet red bell pepper, seeded and cut into thin strips

2 medium tomatoes, peeled and sliced

*I am not sure when or where I discovered that tender summer shoots on pumpkin plants were edible, but finding a recipe was difficult. As a last resort, I was going to try the recipe for fried hop shoots that appears in my great-grandfather's 1872 copy of* **La Cuisine Classique** *by Dubois and Bernard. In this the shoots are lightly blanched, drained, rolled in some flour and egg and fried. However, my sister-in-law told me that the chef from the Indian Ocean restaurant in Brecon, Lukman Miah, was going to show them how to cook pumpkin shoots. The following is the result of her notes.*

1 Peel the stringy bits from the stems of the shoots. Remove any tendrils and chop in half. Wash carefully and let soak in warm water.

2 Heat the oil in a heavy-bottomed medium saucepan over medium-low heat. Sauté the garlic, then the onion until transluscent. Add the salt, cardamom, and 1 cup/250ml of water and bring to a boil.

3 Simmer, uncovered, for 15 minutes or until reduced.

4 Add the curry powder, stir, and cook for 5 minutes. Add another ½ cup/125ml of water.

5 Strain the shoots and add to the saucepan. Simmer until tender — they will take on the color of curry.

6 Add the cilantro and pepper and simmer, uncovered, to reduce the liquid. Add the sliced tomatoes and toss just until heated through.

7 Serve with rice.

# Cooking with Flowers

The blossoms of pumpkin and squash are all edible and can be used in the kitchen in a variety of ways. The simplest is to include them in salads where they make a huge splash of bright yellow color. They are also highly decorative cooked in risotto. Most frequently, flowers are stuffed or fried in batter. Pumpkin seeds can be included in breads or salads, or they can be eaten as a snack, roasted in salt.

## Stuffed Zucchini Flowers

Serves 6

¼ cup/60g long-grain rice

1 small onion, peeled and finely chopped

2 ounces/60g slab or thick-sliced bacon, rind removed, and chopped

3 tablespoons/45g butter, plus more for the baking dish

1 teaspoon chopped fresh thyme

2 medium tomatoes, peeled, seeded, and chopped

8 mini zucchini (2 to 3 inches/5 to 7½ cm long) with flower attached

¼ cup/30g grated Gruyère cheese

salt and freshly ground black pepper

*Zucchini flowers can be stuffed with a variety of things, from cream cheese to tuna, spinach, chicken, or sausage meat. This recipe includes rice and bacon. Pumpkin flowers can also be stuffed and are more suitable used as a main dish.*

1  Preheat the oven to 325°F/170°C and butter an 11x7-inch/27x17-cm baking dish.
2  In a medium saucepan of boiling salted water, cook the rice until just tender (about 20 minutes). Drain, rinse in cold water (to stop it cooking), and drain again.
3  In a small skillet, over medium heat, melt 2 tablespoons of the butter, and fry the onion and bacon until the bacon is crisp.
4  Stir the onion, bacon, pan drippings, thyme, and tomato into the rice. Season to taste with salt and pepper and set aside while you prepare the zucchini with flowers attached.
5  Wash and drain the zucchini with flowers. Pat dry with a towel and trim the ends. Stuff the flower of each one carefully with about a teaspoon of the rice mixture and lay in the baking dish. Season the zucchini with a big pinch of salt and pepper and sprinkle with cheese. Dot with the remaining tablespoon of butter.
6  Bake for 15 minutes, or until the zucchini are tender and the stuffing is heated through.

# Fried Zucchini or Pumpkin Flowers

Serves 8

16 fresh zucchini or pumpkin flowers

2 eggs

salt and freshly ground black pepper

about 2 cups/240g bread crumbs

2 cups/½ liter olive oil

*This makes a very good appetizer, with prosciutto or Parmesan cheese. For the best flavor, use a mix of extra virgin and ordinary olive oil for the frying — from equal parts to 3:1 if you are feeling really extravagant.*

1 Clean the flowers with a wet cloth.

2 Beat the eggs in a small bowl with a little salt and pepper. Put the bread crumbs in another bowl.

3 Dip one flower at a time into the egg and coat with bread crumbs. Do this twice.

4 Heat the oil to a high temperature (hot enough to turn a small piece of bread a golden color soon after dropping it in) in a large heavy-bottomed skillet and cook the flowers, turning them until golden all over.

5 Remove them with a slotted spoon and drain on paper towels. Serve immediately.

# Risotto con Zucchine e Fiori

Serves 6

4½ cups/1 liter chicken broth

3 tablespoons extra virgin olive oil

¼ cup (½ stick)/50g butter

1 small onion (preferably red) or 4 shallots, peeled and chopped

1 garlic clove, peeled and chopped

6 medium zucchini, sliced

10 zucchini flowers, sliced lengthwise through the flower

1½ cups/330g risotto rice, such as Arborio

½ cup/125ml dry white wine

1 cup/100g grated Parmesan cheese

handful of chopped fresh parsley

salt to taste

1 Bring the broth to a boil in a medium saucepan.

2 In a large heavy-bottomed saucepan, heat the oil and a tablespoon of butter over medium-high heat. Sauté the onion and garlic until golden brown. Stir in a ladleful of broth.

3 Add the zucchini and flowers and bring to a simmer. Reduce the heat, cover, and cook for about 10 minutes. If too dry at any stage, add some more broth.

4 Stir in the rice and cook for a few minutes, stirring all the time, until the grains begin to turn translucent. Then add the wine and stir until it is absorbed.

5 Slowly add the broth, keeping the rice moist all the time and stirring slowly. About 15 minutes after adding the rice (or 3-4 minutes before it is cooked), remove the pan from the heat. Add the rest of the butter, the cheese, and the parsley. Stir slowly, being careful to keep the rice moist. Taste and season with salt.

6 Cover and let rest until the rice is soft and tender.

7 Serve immediately.

# Spicy Pumpkin Flowers

4 male pumpkin flowers (*see* page18)

2 garlic cloves, peeled

1 teaspoon turmeric

1 teaspoon mild curry powder

1½ teaspoons dried fenugreek or ground cardamom

½ teaspoon salt

⅓ cup/40g all-purpose flour

vegetable oil for frying

1 Cut the green base from the flowers, slice the flowers in two lengthwise, and remove the anthers (*see* page 18). Wash the flowers carefully and lay out to dry on paper towels.

2 Finely chop one of the garlic cloves and slice the other.

3 In a large bowl, mix the chopped garlic, spices, salt, and flour and add 2 cups/500ml of water. Beat to a batter consistency and stir in the flowers. Let stand.

4 Pour 1 inch/2½ cm of oil in a deep heavy skillet. Heat over medium heat until very hot (hot enough to turn a small piece of bread a golden color soon after dropping it in). Add the sliced garlic to the oil and sauté briefly, just until golden. Remove with a slotted spoon and discard. Then, either add the pumpkin flowers all at once, in which case they will stick together like an omelet, or fry them one at a time until the batter is cooked. It should be crisp around the outside and soft inside. Test by pressing down with a spatula.

5 Drain on paper towels and serve immediately.

# Pumpkin Seeds

Pumpkin seeds make a nutritious snack. To separate the seeds from the fibrous pulp: Soak them for 1 hour in cold water then rinse and drain them in a colander. Scatter the seeds on a baking sheet in a single layer and bake at 300°F/150°C for 30–45 minutes, checking to be sure they are not browning, and shaking the pan a few times. If you like, sprinkle the warm seeds with coarse salt. You may also shell the seeds (making *pepitas*) and use them in recipes for breads, salads, and soups. Store roasted seeds in an airtight container or jar.

Note: The roasting process is necessary to destroy protein toxins in the seeds which can cause sickness. Just a few raw seeds are not going to cause any harm though.

# Salads

Zucchini and summer squash make wonderful summery salads. They can be combined with many different ingredients and tossed in a variety of dressings. One of my favorite salads is a combination of crispy green lettuce and sliced zucchini with a generous helping of blue cheese dressing. Winter squash can also be pressed into service in colder months with delicious results. Here are just a few ideas.

## Zucchini and Leek Salad with Warm Goat Cheese

Serves 4

2 small leeks, with most of the green trimmed away

8 small zucchini or 4 medium ones, thinly sliced

⅖ cup/50g chopped walnuts

8 ounces/250g soft goat cheese, cubed

for the dressing:

1 tablespoon red wine vinegar

3 tablespoons walnut oil

½ teaspoon whole-grain mustard

salt and freshly ground black pepper

*An excellent starter that goes with meat, fish, or poultry menus, this salad includes a little warm cheese. Any soft cheese covered with an edible rind can be used, but goat's cheese has a distinctive taste that stands out from the zucchini and leek.*

1 Blanch both the leeks and zucchini in a pot of boiling salted water for 1 minute, then drain. Dry the zucchini. Slice the leeks across into rounds.

2 Make the dressing by whisking together the ingredients in a small bowl with salt and pepper to taste. Pour the dressing over the leeks and zucchini while they are still warm. Toss in the walnuts.

3 Just before you are ready to serve the salad, heat the broiler. Place the cheese cubes in a foil-lined pan or metal pie plate and broil for a couple of minutes until barely melting and toss it into the salad.

4 Serve immediately.

# Zucchini, Yellow Pepper, and Mushroom Salad

Serves 4

8 small zucchini, thinly sliced
1 medium yellow bell pepper, seeded and diced
8 ounces/225g button mushrooms, sliced

for the dressing:
¼ teaspoon dry mustard
1 tablespoon white wine vinegar
3 tablespoons olive oil
2 garlic cloves, finely chopped
salt and freshly ground black pepper

1 Blanch the zucchini in a pot of boiling salted water for 1 minute. Drain in a colander and refresh under cold running water. Dry well with a clean cloth or paper towel. Put in a salad bowl and mix with the bell pepper and mushrooms.
2 Make the dressing by whisking the ingredients in a small bowl with salt and pepper to taste. Pour it over the salad and toss to mix.
3 Chill in the refrigerator for 30 minutes before serving.

# Zucchini Salad

Serves 4

8 small zucchini, finely diced
2 handfuls of chopped fresh parsley or cilantro
1 hard-cooked egg, finely chopped

for the dressing:
1 teaspoon Dijon mustard
1 tablespoon red wine vinegar
3 tablespoons olive oil
salt and freshly ground black pepper

1 Mix the zucchini and parsley or cilantro in a large serving bowl.
2 Make the dressing by whisking the ingredients in a small bowl with salt and pepper to taste. Pour it over the salad and toss to mix.
3 Garnish the salad with the egg.

# Cold Pasta with Zucchini and Tomatoes

Serves 4-6

12 ounces/330g conchiglie (shell pasta)
salt
3 medium zucchini
12 cherry tomatoes, quartered
4 ounces/125g mozzarella cheese, cubed
⅔ cup/165ml ricotta, at room temperature
handful of parsley, chopped
3 tablespoons olive oil

1 Cook the pasta in a large pot of boiling salted water until *al dente*. Drain in a colander, rinse under cold water, and let cool completely.
2 Meanwhile, cook the whole zucchini in boiling water that barely covers them for 5–10 minutes, until tender. Slice and allow to cool completely.
3 In a large bowl, mix the pasta, zucchini, tomatoes, cheeses, parsley, olive oil, and season with salt to taste. Serve cold.

# Winter Squash and Apple Salad

1 pound/500g winter squash, peeled, seeded and cut into ¾-inch/2-cm cubes

2 crunchy apples

juice of 1 medium lemon

½ cup/60g golden raisins

⅔ cup/60g walnut pieces

for the dressing:

2 tablespoons mayonnaise

2 tablespoons plain yogurt

¼ teaspoon Dijon mustard

½ teaspoon honey

salt and freshly ground black pepper

*Chunks of cooked pumpkin and winter squash lend real substance to salad. For this recipe choose a winter squash variety that has firm and dry flesh, such as hubbard or butternut squash.*

1 Steam the squash pieces in a steamer basket over barely simmering water for about 10 minutes. They should be just tender and still in firm cubes.

2 Core and slice the apples and toss the apple slices in lemon juice.

3 Make the dressing by whisking together all the ingredients with salt and pepper to taste in a small bowl.

4 In a large bowl, mix the squash, apples, golden raisins, and walnut pieces. Carefully stir in the dressing without breaking the squash pieces.

5 Chill for half an hour before serving.

# Delicata Squash and Lentil Salad

½ cup/200g brown lentils

1 medium 'Delicata' squash peeled, seeded, and sliced

3 tablespoons finely chopped fresh parsley

2 tablespoons finely chopped fresh chives

1 tablespoon finely chopped fresh tarragon

2 ounces/60g red Leicester, Gouda, sharp Cheddar, or any other hard tasty cheese, cut into 1½-inch/1-cm cubes

1 large green bell pepper, seeded and chopped

12 black olives, pitted

for the dressing:

¼ cup/60ml cider vinegar

⅓ cup/90ml vegetable oil

1 tablespoon finely chopped shallots

salt and freshly ground black pepper

1 Put the lentils in a saucepan with 4½ cups/1 liter water. Bring to a boil over high heat, skimming if necessary. Reduce the heat, cover, and let simmer for about 35 minutes or until tender. Drain and let cool completely. Season to taste with salt.

2 At the same time, in a large saucepan, cook the squash slices in boiling water for 20–25 minutes, until just tender. Drain and let cool slightly.

3 Make the dressing: In a small bowl, whisk together the vinegar, oil, and shallots with salt and pepper to taste. Set half of it to one side and mix the herbs with the rest.

4 While the squash is still warm, arrange it around a large flat dish and spoon over the herb-flavored dressing.

5 When the lentils are cold, mix them in a bowl with the reserved dressing. Pile in the center of the dish.

6 Decorate the base of the lentils, where they meet the squash, with the cheese cubes, bell pepper, and olives.

# Breads & Baking

Few aromas beat that of home baking, whether the dough is leavened with baker's yeast or baking powder. Most of the recipes included here require few ingredients and are easy to make — it is just a question of building in the time for allowing the dough to rise if yeast has been used.

## Pumpkin Tea Bread

2⅔ cups/360g self-rising flour
½ teaspoon baking soda
1 teaspoon ground cinnamon
½ teaspoon freshly grated nutmeg
½ teaspoon ground allspice
½ cup (1 stick)/125g butter, cut into bits
⅔ cup/125g granulated sugar
2 tablespoons golden syrup or light corn syrup
1 cup/250ml pumpkin purée
1 cup/250ml milk, preferably buttermilk

*This not-too-sweet spicy bread is ideal for serving with mid-morning coffee or afternoon tea. It can be eaten as it is or spread with butter, and has the advantage of keeping well in an airtight container.*

1  Preheat the oven to 375°F/190°C. Grease a 9x5-inch/23x13-cm loaf pan.
2  In a large bowl, stir together the flour, baking soda, and spices. Cut in the butter until the mixture resembles cornmeal. Stir in the sugar.
3  In a medium bowl, whisk together the golden syrup, pumpkin, and milk and add to the flour mix. Beat with a spoon just until all the ingredients are incorporated, but for as short a time as possible. The consistency of the mixture should be quite stiff.
4  Turn into the prepared pan and bake for 50 minutes to 1 hour, or until the loaf is well-risen, browned, and a toothpick inserted in the center comes out clean.
5  Transfer to a wire rack and let cool for 30 minutes. Turn out of the pan and cool completely on the rack.

# Pumpkin Bread

6½ cups/780g bread flour, plus extra for kneading

1 envelope quick-rising yeast

2 teaspoons salt

1¼ cup/310ml pumpkin purée

1 cup/250ml very hot water

butter for the pan

*This recipe is based on the one I use every week for our household bread. I normally use whole wheat flour, but I feel that the lighter consistency given by white flour is better in combination with pumpkin. However, variations are numerous; see below.*

*The drier the pumpkin purée, the more liquid is required to make the dough. The pumpkin imparts a beautiful orange color to the bread. Pumpkin bread freezes well.*

1  In a large bowl, stir together the flour, yeast, and salt.

2  Warm the pumpkin purée and stir it into the flour mixture. Add the water a little at a time, until enough is incorporated to make a soft but slightly sticky dough. The exact quantity will depend on the water content of the pumpkin purée.

3  Turn the dough out onto a lightly floured surface and knead for 6–8 minutes, adding a bit of flour, if necessary, until smooth and elastic. Let the dough rest on the work surface for 10 minutes.

4  Butter well a 9x5-inch/23x13-cm loaf pan. Pat or roll the dough into a 10x12-inch/25x30-cm rectangle about ½ inch/1cm thick. Beginning with a short side, tightly roll up the dough and tuck the edges under. Place the dough seam-side down in the prepared pan (pan will be about ⅔ full).

5  Cover loosely with a damp cloth or oiled plastic wrap. Leave in a warm place to rise until about 1 inch/2½ cm over the rim of the pan — this can take from 1–2 hours, depending on how warm the room, implements, and ingredients are.

6  Preheat the oven to 400°F/200°C. Bake the loaf for 30 minutes. Remove carefully from the pan and return to the oven upside down, to allow the bottom and sides to crisp up, about 6 minutes. The loaf is cooked when it sounds hollow when tapped at the base.

**Variations**  Instead of white flour only, use half white and half whole wheat or only whole wheat. Remember whole wheat flour tends to require more liquid. To vary the taste, add ground cinnamon, nutmeg, and ginger to the flour, or add herbs like thyme and chives. A little sugar could also be added.

Instead of water, use a mixture of water and milk or just milk for a softer result. Alternatively, eggs can be used in lieu of some of the liquid for a richer bread.

Many people rub 2 tablespoons/30g of butter or margarine into the flour or add 2 tablespoons of olive oil to the liquid. This improves the keeping qualities of the bread, although I never find the bread lasts long enough to warrant doing it.

# Zucchini and Carrot Loaf

1 tablespoon olive oil

1 small onion, finely chopped

1 egg

2 cups/250g coarsely grated zucchini

1½ cups/125g coarsely grated carrot

¼ cup (½ stick)/60g butter, melted, plus more for the pan

3 cups/350g bread flour, plus more for dusting

1 envelope quick-rising yeast

1 teaspoon salt

*This is not a sandwich bread, rather it is a moist, dense, flavorful loaf which is delicious warm with a mixed salad, soup, or soft, mild cheese.*

1  Heat the olive oil in a small skillet and sauté the onion until translucent.

2  In a large bowl, beat the egg and mix in the zucchini, carrot, melted butter, and sautéd onion. Add the flour, yeast, and salt and stir to mix. Work with your hands for about 1 minute, until the dough comes together and forms a ball.

3  Butter well an 8½x4½-inch/21x11-cm loaf pan and dust it with flour. Pat the dough into the prepared pan. Cover with a damp cloth or an oiled piece of plastic wrap and let rise in a warm place for 1½–2 hours until doubled in size; the exact time will depend on the temperature of the ingredients, bowl, and room.

4  Preheat the oven to 400°F/200°C.

5  Bake for about 40 minutes, or until golden brown.

6  Turn out on a rack and allow to cool slightly.

# Pumpkin Scones

2 cups/250g self-rising flour

2 cups/250g whole wheat flour

¾ teaspoon baking soda

½ cup (1 stick)/125g cold butter, cut into bits

½ cup/100g granulated sugar

½ cup/60g golden raisins

½ cup/125ml pumpkin purée

1 cup/250ml milk, preferably buttermilk

milk for brushing

*Scones are great standbys as they are quick to make and freeze very well. These are particularly light and moist. Serve them with butter or cream cheese.*

1  Preheat the oven to 425°F/220°C. Dust 2 baking sheets with flour.

2  Stir together the flours and baking soda in a large bowl.

3  Cut in the butter until the mixture resembles cornmeal. Stir in the sugar and golden raisins. Mix in the pumpkin purée first with a spoon then with your hands.

4  Add just enough buttermilk to make a soft dough, kneading it briefly in the bowl. (Dough will be crumbly.) Don't handle it for too long.

5  Roll out on a floured board to a thickness of about 1 inch/2½cm and cut into rounds with a floured 2-inch/5-cm cutter. Reroll and cut scraps once.

6  Place on prepared baking sheets and brush with milk. Bake for 10–15 minutes, or until well risen and golden brown.

7  Allow to cool on a wire rack.

# Pumpkin Pies

North Americans make the best pies – whether apple, pecan, or pumpkin — and many households have their own recipe which has been handed down through the generations from mother to daughter. There are many variations on the theme including the French recipe below and one of my favorites, a pumpkin meringue pie. The early Australian settlers also used to make a closed pie which simply included pumpkin, butter, sugar, and lemon, and was evocatively called Outback Pie.

## Pumpkin and Almond Pie

Serves 6-8

one 17½-ounce package puff pastry sheets thawed and unfolded according to package directions, or 1 pound/500g puff pastry

1 cup/250ml pumpkin purée

½ cup/90g granulated sugar

¼ cup (½ stick)/60g butter, at room temperature

1¼ cups/125g ground almonds

1 beaten egg, plus more for glazing

1 tablespoon lemon juice

*Several versions of pumpkin tarts and pie are indigenous to the south of France, where they are mostly served on festive occasions. They all include ground almonds which are plentiful in the region. This not-too-sweet pie is a welcome addition to any holiday table.*

1  Preheat the oven to 450°F/230°C.

2  Roll out each sheet of the pastry to a thickness of ⅛ inch/¼ cm. From each sheet cut out a circle about 8 inches/20cm across. Place one on a dampened baking sheet. Roll the other circle out to about 9 inches/23 cm. Leave in a cold place. Wrap and refrigerate scraps to use at another time.

3  In a small bowl, combine the pumpkin purée with about 2½ tablespoons/30g of the sugar.

4  With an electric mixer at medium-high speed, cream the butter with the remaining sugar until light and fluffy. Add the ground almonds, egg, and lemon juice. Beat thoroughly.

5  Spread the pumpkin on the smaller round of pastry, leaving a border of about ½ inch/ 1½ cm. Heap the almond-butter mixture on top, making a dome in the center.

6  Brush the pastry border with beaten egg and cover with the larger circle of pastry. Press down all the way round the edge with your thumb to seal and glaze the top with beaten egg. Make 8 slashes in the lid, approximately 3 inches/8cm long — rather like spokes of a wheel that neither meet in the center nor reach the edge of the wheel.

7  Bake for 25–30 minutes, or until well-risen, cooked, and golden. Allow to cool on a wire rack.

# Pumpkin Pie

for the pie pastry:

2 cups plus 1 tablespoon/250g all-purpose flour

¼ teaspoon salt

¼ cup (½ stick)/60g cold stick margarine, cut into bits

¼ cup/60g solid white vegetable shortening

about ⅓ cup/85ml cold water

for the filling :

2 eggs

1¼ cups/200g packed light brown sugar

¼ cup (½ stick)/60g butter, melted

¼ teaspoon salt

1 teaspoon vanilla extract

1½ cups/375ml pumpkin purée

½ cup/125ml light cream

*Pumpkin pie is a classic North American dessert that has been made since the days of the Pilgrims. It usually contains eggs, milk or cream (or evaporated milk, which I do not favor), sugar, and spices — in various combinations and quantities, depending on taste.*

*Traditionally, pumpkin pie is made in a deep pie dish, but I like to make it in a shallow (1 inch/2½ cm deep) 9-inch/23-cm loose-bottomed quiche or tart pan. If you are using a fresh pumpkin purée, it should always be well thickened by cooking on low heat, stirring frequently to avoid burning. Canned pumpkin (not pumpkin pie filling) works well, if you don't have fresh.*

*The pie pastry recipe is one I learned as a child and use for most pies, tarts, and quiches. It produces light and flavorful pastry. Here it is in alliance with my own favorite filling: a rich sweet pudding in which the taste of the pumpkin is enhanced by the flavor of vanilla extract.*

1 First make the pastry (be sure that all the ingredients and your hands are cold): Stir together the flour and salt in a large bowl and add the margarine and shortening. Gently rub in the fat until the mixture resembles cornmeal, moving your hands up and down all of the time to incorporate as much air as possible.

2 Adding as little of the water as is necessary (but without worrying too much) and using a knife at first and then your fingers, lightly work the mixture together to make a ball. Pat it carefully to make sure it all sticks together. Wrap it in plastic wrap and chill in the refrigerator for 30 minutes.

3 On a floured surface (a piece of floured marble is ideal), roll out the pastry with long firm strokes until it makes a circle a little under 12 inches/30cm across. Using the rolling pin, lift and transfer it to line a 9-inch/23-cm loose-bottomed tart pan. Don't worry if it breaks, you can always stick it together or patch it up with a little water or pastry trimmings. Push the pastry down a little around the edge to make a thicker border. Trim the edge. Chill again for about 30 minutes or until required.

4 Preheat the oven to 400°F/200°C. Fit the pastry shell with foil, fill with beans or pie weights, and bake blind for 10 minutes, or until the crust just starts to turn golden at the edges. Remove to a wire rack to cool. Increase the oven temperature to 450°F/230°C.

5 Make the filling: In a medium bowl, whisk together the eggs, sugar, butter, salt, and vanilla until smooth. Whisk in the pumpkin and cream.

6 Place the tart pan on a baking sheet. Pour the filling into the prepared pie crust and bake for 10 minutes. Reduce the oven setting to 350°F/180°C and bake for 40–45 minutes, or until the filling is almost set. Transfer to a wire rack to cool. It will continue to cook a little while cooling down.

7 Serve with *crème fraîche*, or unsweetened softly whipped cream which will provide an ideal foil for the sweetness of the pie. Refrigerate leftovers.

# Mike's Breakfast Pumpkin Pie

Serves 6-8

1 recipe pie pastry, chilled
(*see* Pumpkin Pie, page 90)

2½ cups/625ml pumpkin purée

1 cup/170g granulated sugar

1 teaspoon ground cinnamon

1 tablespoon freshly grated ginger

3 eggs, lightly beaten

1½ cups/375ml milk

*Mike's Breakfast is an expatriates' haven in Kathmandu where one can retreat from the hurly-burly of the busy town and enjoy a delicious, simple meal. Mike gave me the following recipe, in which he uses the native pumpkin; those grown from seed brought back from the West do not withstand the monsoon conditions.*

1 Preheat the oven to 450°F/230°C. Line a 9-inch/23-cm pie pan with the pastry and crimp the edges.

2 In a medium bowl, whisk together the pumpkin, sugar, and spices. Add the eggs and milk and beat well. Pour into the pie shell.

3 Bake for 10 minutes, reduce the oven setting to 350°F/180°C and bake for 40 minutes longer, until the center of the filling is just set. Remove to a wire rack to cool. Serve with cream sweetened with maple syrup, or vanilla ice cream. Refrigerate leftovers.

# Pumpkin Meringue Pie

Serves 6-8

for the rich shortcrust pastry:

1½ cups/180g all-purpose flour

2 teaspoons granulated sugar

½ cup (1 stick)/125g cold butter, cut into bits

1 egg yolk

for the filling and meringue:

3 tablespoons/30g cornstarch

¼ cup/60ml milk

1 cup/250ml pumpkin purée

2 tablespoons/30g granulated sugar

2 tablespoons/30g butter

2 eggs, separated

grated zest and juice of 1 medium lemon

⅔ cup/125g superfine sugar

1 First make the rich shortcrust pastry (be sure that all the ingredients and your hands are cold): Sift the flour and sugar into a large bowl and add the butter. Gently rub in the butter until the mixture resembles cornmeal, moving your hands up and down all of the time to incorporate as much air as possible. Stir in the egg yolk and a little cold water a tablespoon at a time if necessary to mix to a smooth dough. Pat it carefully into a ball to make sure it all sticks together. Wrap it in plastic wrap and chill in the refrigerator for 30 minutes.

2 On a floured surface (a piece of floured marble is ideal), roll out the pastry with long firm strokes until it makes a circle a little under 12 inches/30cm across. Using the rolling pin, lift and transfer it to line a 9-inch/23-cm loose-bottomed tart pan. Refrigerate until ready to use.

3 Preheat the oven to 300°F/150°C.

4 For the filling: In a medium heavy-bottomed saucepan, mix the cornstarch smoothly with the milk and mix in the pumpkin purée. Cook on high heat, stirring constantly for 3–4 minutes, until it begins to thicken. Add the sugar and butter, and remove from the heat; let cool for 10 minutes. Beat in the egg yolks, lemon zest and juice.

5 Make the meringue by beating the egg whites in a large bowl with an electric mixer until soft peaks form. Whisk in 1 tablespoon of the superfine sugar. Then fold in the remainder gradually, until whites are stiff and glossy.

7 Pour the pumpkin mixture into the pastry shell and heap the meringue over the top. Spread it right to the edge of the pastry, sealing in the pumpkin completely.

6 Bake for 40 minutes, or until the meringue is pale brown and crispy on the outside.

8 Serve warm or cold. Refrigerate leftovers.

# Cakes & Cookies

Pumpkin purée works wonders in cakes and cookies. It is light and moist and imparts a lovely orange color to the end results. By combining it with different ingredients, you can vary the character of baked goods from fruity to spicy to creamy. The recipe below is the exception in this chapter. It uses zucchini for surprisingly delicious results.

## Chocolate Zucchini Snack Cake

Makes 12 squares

½ cup/30g unsweetened cocoa powder
1 tablespoon instant coffee
½ cup/125ml hot water
1 cup/215g packed light brown sugar
2 eggs, at room temperature
½ cup/125ml vegetable oil
1 cup/160g zucchini, finely grated
4 ounces/100g semisweet chocolate, melted
½ cup/60g whole wheat flour
2½ cups/285g all-purpose flour
1¾ teaspoons baking powder
½ teaspoon baking soda
½ teaspoon salt

*This recipe is a real puzzler for anyone trying it for the first time. Rich in chocolate, wonderfully moist and nutty, but there are no nuts and the zucchini is unidentifiable!*

1  Preheat the oven to 350°F/180°C. Grease an 8-inch/20-cm square cake pan: Line the bottom with waxed paper and grease the paper.

2  Dissolve the cocoa and coffee in the hot water and let cool.

3  In a large bowl, whisk together the sugar, eggs, and oil until smooth. Stir in the zucchini and melted chocolate. In a medium bowl, stir together the flours, baking powder, baking soda, and salt. Add the flour mixture to the chocolate mixture and stir to blend. The batter will be stiff.

4  Turn the mixture into the prepared pan and bake for 50 minutes, or until the top springs back when gently touched and a toothpick inserted in the center comes out clean.

5  Let cool for 5 minutes before turning out onto a wire rack. Remove paper from bottom.

6  For a double-chocolate flavor, drizzle the cake with melted milk or white chocolate. Cut into squares to serve.

# Pumpkin Fruit Cake

Makes 15 slices

½ cup (1 stick)/125g butter, at room temperature, plus more for the pan

⅔ cup/125g packed light brown sugar

2 eggs

2 cups plus 1 tablespoon/250g self-rising flour, sifted

¼ teaspoon baking soda

½ cup/125ml pumpkin purée

grated zest and juice of 1 medium lemon

⅔ cup/100g golden raisins

¾ cup/100g dried apricots, chopped

¾ cup/100g dried peaches, chopped

⅔ cup/60g walnuts, chopped

for the lemon frosting:

3 tablespoons sifted confectioners' sugar

2 teaspoons lemon juice

*This nutritious cake is ideal for packing in a lunch box or for taking on a picnic. The combination of fruit is unusual and gives a fresh taste which reminds one of summer.*

1  Preheat the oven to 350°F/180°C and butter a 10x4-inch/25x11-cm tube pan.

2  With an electric mixer at medium-high speed, cream the butter and sugar. Beat in the eggs. By hand, with a rubber spatula, fold in the flour, baking soda, pumpkin, lemon zest and juice. Then gently incorporate the fruit and nuts.

3  Turn the mixture into the prepared cake pan and bake for 40–45 minutes or until a toothpick inserted in the center comes out clean.

4  Remove from the oven, let the cake cool in the pan on a wire rack for 5 minutes and then turn it out onto the rack.

5  When it is quite cool, spread the top with lemon frosting made by mixing the confectioners' sugar with the lemon juice.

# Pumpkin Cornbread Muffins

Makes 12

1½ cups/180g all-purpose flour

½ cup plus 1 tablespoon/90g cornmeal

1 tablespoon baking powder

¼ teaspoon baking soda

¼ teaspoon salt

1 teaspoon ground cinnamon

½ teaspoon ground mace

¼ cup/60g granulated sugar

1 egg

2 tablespoons/30g butter, melted, plus more for the pan

½ cup/125ml milk

zest and juice of 1 medium orange

1 cup/250ml pumpkin purée

*The addition of cornmeal in this recipe gives a slightly crunchy, open texture. The secret of good muffins is in the speed and efficiency of combining the dry and wet ingredients. Too many strokes cause the gluten in the flour to develop and make the muffin tough.*

1  Preheat the oven to 400°F/200°C and butter a muffin pan well.

2  In a large bowl, stir together the flour, cornmeal, baking powder, baking soda, salt, spices, and sugar.

3  In a medium bowl, whisk together the egg, butter, milk, orange zest and juice, and pumpkin purée.

4  Pour the wet ingredients over the dry and in as few movements as possible, combine the two. Don't worry about the lumps — they will cook out.

5  Spoon the mixture into the prepared muffin pan.

6  Bake for 20 minutes or until browned and springy to the touch. Remove from the oven and allow to cool in the pan on a wire rack for 5 minutes. Then turn out and allow to cool completely on a wire rack.

# Pumpkin Honey Oatmeal Cookies

Makes about 66

2 cups/250g self-rising flour

½ teaspoon baking soda

¾ cup (1½ sticks)/180g cold butter, cut into bits, plus more for the baking sheets

2 cups/180g old-fashioned oats

¾ cup/170g packed light brown sugar

½ cup/125ml pumpkin purée

¼ cup/60ml honey

*Homemade cookies are always a treat, particularly for children. They'll love these chunky, chewy treats.*

1  Preheat the oven to 375°F/190°C and butter several baking sheets well.
2  In a large bowl, stir together the flour and baking soda. Rub in the butter until the mixture resembles cornmeal. Mix in the oatmeal and sugar, crumbling any lumps with your fingers. Then stir in the pumpkin purée and honey. Work the dough together with your hands.
3  Shape the dough into balls about the size of walnuts. Place these on the prepared baking sheets, spacing them about 2 inches/5cm apart.
4  Bake for 9–11 minutes, until golden brown.
5  Let cool for a minute before transferring cookies to a wire rack to cool completely.

Note: If you are unable to cook all the dough at once, keep it refrigerated while waiting for space in the oven.

# Pumpkin Cheesecake

Serves 6-8

for the crust:

¼ cup (½ stick)/60g butter

7 ounces (2½ cups small cookies)/200g gingersnaps, finely crushed

8 ounces/250g mascarpone cheese

8 ounces (1 cup)/250g ricotta cheese

2 cups/500ml dry pumpkin purée (*see page 72*)

½ cup/60g confectioners' sugar

grated zest of 1 medium lemon and juice of ½ of it

2 envelopes/15g gelatin

*This rich cheesecake is not too sweet and can be served with coffee for a mid-morning break or as a dessert. The pumpkin purée should not be too wet or the cake will not set successfully.*

1  Melt the butter in a medium saucepan, remove from heat, and mix in the crushed gingersnaps. Press the mixture into the bottom of an 8- or 9-inch/20- or 23-cm loose-bottomed or springform pan, making sure it is solid and level. Chill for 20 minutes.
2  With an electric mixer at medium speed, beat the mascarpone and ricotta cheeses together until as smooth as possible. With mixer at low speed, beat in the pumpkin, sugar, lemon zest, and juice.
3  Put 2 tablespoons of cold water in a bowl and sprinkle the gelatin over. Give it one stir and leave for about 5 minutes, or until spongy. Place the bowl over hot water (or put the gelatin in a saucepan over low heat) and stir until the gelatin is dissolved — it will turn clear. Whisk the gelatin quickly into the pumpkin mixture.
4  Pour into the crust and spread to the edges. Cover and chill until set, about 2 hours.

# Other Desserts

Many of my friends think the only dessert that is made from pumpkin is pie, so I like to surprise them with other possibilities. Some of the more unusual desserts are very sweet and need only be served in small quantities. Others, such as the steamed pudding, are based on more traditional recipes.

## Pumpkin Ice Cream

Serves 6-8

6 egg yolks
1¼ cups/250g superfine sugar
½ cup/125ml pumpkin purée
1 teaspoon lemon juice
1⅓ cups/300ml heavy cream

*An easy way to make pumpkin ice cream is to fold the pumpkin and sugar (and a pinch of nutmeg or pumpkin pie spice, if desired) into some softened vanilla ice cream. This recipe contains eggs and cream that are combined with pumpkin, whipped cream, and sugar to make a rich, smooth dessert.*

1  In the top of a double boiler, over simmering water, whisk the egg yolks and sugar for 10–15 minutes, until thick and creamy. Remove from the heat.
2  Gradually whisk in the pumpkin purée and lemon juice. Transfer to a large bowl.
3  In a separate bowl, by hand with a wire whisk or with an electric mixer at high speed, beat the cream until just forming soft peaks. Fold the cream into the pumpkin mixture.
4  Transfer into a 6-cup/1½-liter freezer container, cover, and freeze for at least 4 hours.
5  To serve, allow to thaw at room temperature for 10–15 minutes or until the desired consistency and accompany with gingersnaps.

# Anardi

⅔ cup/125g superfine sugar

4 cups/1 liter dry pumpkin purée

3 egg whites

1⅓ cups/150g ground almonds

grated zest of 1 medium lemon

½ cup/75g sliced unblanched almonds

butter for the baking sheet

for the syrup:

1¼ cups/250g granulated sugar

juice of 1 medium lemon

*This traditional combination of pumpkin and almonds soaked in syrup is typical of Mediterranean countries. It makes a deliciously sweet ending to a meal. Small quantities only are required!*

1  Preheat the oven to 375°F/190°C and butter a baking sheet.

2  In a large bowl, mix the superfine sugar with the pumpkin and gradually beat in the egg whites. Stir in the ground almonds and lemon zest. Work the mixture until you have a stiff dough.

3  Place the dough on the buttered baking sheet, giving it a domed shape, and cover with the sliced almonds.

4  Bake for 50 minutes.

5  Make the syrup by dissolving the cup of granulated sugar in ½ cup/125ml water with the lemon juice in a medium saucepan. Bring to a boil over high heat, reduce heat to medium, and simmer for 5 minutes.

6  Transfer the cake to a rimmed serving dish and pour the syrup over the cake while still hot. Leave to soak up the syrup while it cools.

# Steamed Pumpkin Pudding

1 cup/125g self-rising flour

1 teaspoon freshly grated nutmeg

¼ cup (½ stick)/60g cold butter or margarine, cut into bits, plus more for the mold

1½ cups/125g dry bread crumbs

⅔ cup/125g packed brown sugar

1½ cups/250g golden raisins

2 cups/200g finely grated pumpkin

2 eggs, lightly beaten

*Steamed pudding is a favorite winter dessert in our family. This simple recipe makes a light pudding that melts in the mouth and is always a success.*

1  In a large bowl, stir together the flour and nutmeg.

2  Rub in the butter or margarine until the mixture resembles cornmeal.

3  Stir in the bread crumbs, sugar, and golden raisins, crumbling any lumps of sugar with your fingers. Stir in the grated pumpkin and eggs until well blended.

4  Turn the mixture into a well-buttered 6¼-cup/1½-liter pudding mold, cover with a piece of waxed paper pleated in the center to allow room for expansion. Firmly tie a piece of string around the rim of the bowl to lift it from the pan.

5  Put the bowl in a large saucepan and add boiling water to come halfway up the bowl. Cover tightly and steam for 1½–2 hours, or until firm to the touch, checking the pan from time to time and adding more boiling water as necessary.

6  Unmold and serve hot with brandy-flavored custard sauce.

# Sweet Pumpkin Dessert

Serves 6-8

6 cups/1½ liters pumpkin purée
½ cup/100g light brown sugar
½ cup/100g granulated sugar
¾ cup/175ml kirsch

1  In a large bowl, whisk together the pumpkin purée and the brown sugar. Transfer to a large serving bowl.

2  Make some caramel: In a small heavy-bottomed pan, melt the granulated sugar over moderate heat until it turns brown, stirring occasionally. Carefully pour the caramel over the pumpkin purée.

3  Drench with the kirsch and serve with *crème fraîche*.

# Pumpkin and Orange Roulade

Serves 10-12

1¾ cups/200g self-rising flour
2 teaspoons cinnamon
1 teaspoon mace
3 eggs
⅔ cup/125g granulated sugar
½ cup/125ml pumpkin purée
1 tablespoon orange juice
1½ cups/180g confectioners' sugar, plus extra for rolling
6 ounces/180g cream cheese, at room temperature
¼ cup (½ stick)/60g butter, softened
grated zest and juice of ½ medium orange
4 ounces/100g semisweet chocolate
1 tablespoon/15g butter
1 teaspoon heavy cream

*This rich dessert can be made in advance and is good for a party.*

1  Preheat the oven to 400°F/200°C. Line a jelly-roll pan with a piece of parchment paper or foil.

2  Sift the flour and spices together.

3  In a large bowl, whisk the eggs and sugar until creamy. Then mix in the pumpkin and 1 tablespoon of the orange juice. Carefully fold in the flour.

4  Turn into the prepared pan and bake for 10–15 minutes or until springy to the touch. Let cool 5 minutes on a wire rack.

5  Invert the cake onto a rack, lift off the pan and parchment paper lining. Place a large, dampened cotton or linen tea towel on the counter and place a sheet of waxed paper over that. Dust the waxed paper with a fairly thick layer of confectioners' sugar. Roll together cake, sugared paper, and towel and let cool.

6  With an electric mixer at medium-high speed, beat together the confectioners' sugar, cream cheese, butter, orange zest and juice until smooth and creamy.

7  Unroll the cake and spread with the cream cheese mixture. Roll up the cake again, place seam-side down on a serving dish, cover, and chill.

8  In the top of a double boiler, over barely simmering water, melt the chocolate, butter, and cream, stirring until smooth. Spread the chocolate glaze evenly over the cake and chill until set.

# Pickles & Jellies

It is always satisfying to open the cupboard and see jars of homemade pickles and jams, neatly labeled and in tidy rows. By fall pumpkin and squash can be in plentiful supply, so use the surplus to make some of the following recipes to enjoy when the garden is no longer producing. Remember that the preserve will last longer if the jar has been scrupulously cleaned in hot soapy water or in a dishwasher then sterilized by gently boiling in water to cover by 1 inch/2½cm for 10 minutes. Place lids in a separate small saucepan of water, bring to a simmer, and remove from the heat. Keep both jars and lids in water until just before filling. Yields are for 16-ounce jars.

## Pumpkin and Ginger Pickle

Makes 4-6 jars

1 ounce/30g fresh ginger, a piece about 2 inches/5cm wide and ½ inch/1cm thick

zest of 2 medium lemons, removed with a vegetable peeler

2 pounds/1kg pumpkin, peeled, seeded, and cut into 1-inch/2½-cm cubes

2 large garlic cloves, peeled and finely chopped

1 tablespoon plus 1½ teaspoons/15g kosher salt

½ teaspoon cayenne pepper

3½ cups (1 pound)/500g golden raisins

two 16-ounce boxes/1kg packed dark brown sugar

2 cups/½ liter cider vinegar

*Ginger lends piquancy to this beautifully colored deep orange pickle. Its blend of flavors makes this pickle a good accompaniment to cold turkey, ham, or chicken.*

1  Crush the ginger with a hammer and place it with the lemon in a cheesecloth bag. Tie the bag securely.

2  Put all the ingredients in a large, heavy-bottomed nonaluminum saucepan and bring to a boil over high heat. Reduce the heat and simmer gently, stirring frequently, until the mixture thickens and the pumpkin is tender.

3  Remove the bag of flavorings and spoon the pickle in the sterilized warm jars while hot. Seal when hot; label when cold.

4  Keep for 3 months in the refrigerator before using.

# Rosa Tidy's Pickled Zucchini

Makes 2-3 jars

about 2 tablespoons olive oil

1 pound/500g zucchini, thinly sliced lengthwise

2 garlic cloves, minced

small bunch of fresh mint, finely chopped

about 2 cups/½ liter white wine vinegar

*Rosa Tidy is a cooking instructor, food writer, and friend. Here is her recipe for pickled zucchini, which she recommends serving with cold meats or as a sandwich filling.*

1 Heat the olive oil in a large heavy-bottomed skillet and cook the zucchini until golden on both sides, adding a little more oil if necessary.

2 Remove the zucchini slices from the pan, drain on paper towels, and let cool.

3 Fill sterilized jars with the zucchini, then add the garlic and mint. Top up with vinegar, seal with a lid, and store in the refrigerator.

# Mavis's Summer Squash Piccalilli

Makes 6-8 jars

3 pounds/1½kg yellow crookneck summer squash, peeled, seeded, and cut into small pieces

1 pound/500g onion, peeled and finely chopped

2 pounds/1kg apples, peeled, cored, and cut into small pieces

3½ cups/875ml cider vinegar

one 16-ounce box/500kg packed light or dark brown sugar

1 tablespoon all-purpose flour

1 tablespoon dry mustard

1 tablespoon ground ginger

1 tablespoon ground turmeric

1 tablespoon salt

½ teaspoon cayenne pepper

*This recipe was given to me by food photographer — and fellow pumpkin and squash enthusiast — Tessa Traeger. She, in turn, had been given it by Mavis, her Devon neighbor. It makes the perfect spicy accompaniment to cold meats.*

1 Put the squash, onions, and apples in a large heavy-bottomed nonaluminum saucepan with enough vinegar to cover, bring to a boil over high heat, reduce the heat, and simmer until just soft, about 20 minutes.

2 In a medium bowl, whisk together the sugar, flour, mustard, spices, salt, and cayenne pepper with the remaining vinegar.

3 Pour the vinegar mixture into the vegetables and stir to blend. Continue to simmer gently, stirring, until the flour is cooked and the piccalilli is well mixed, about 5 minutes.

4 Transfer the mixture to warm dry sterilized jars and seal immediately. Cool, label, and store in the refrigerator.

# Squash Chutney

Makes 8-10 jars

5 pounds/2½kg squash, peeled, seeded, and cut into 1-inch/2½-cm cubes

1 pound/500g onions, peeled and chopped

4 medium bananas, peeled and thickly sliced

1¾ cups (8 ounces)/250g raisins

3 cups/750ml cider vinegar

1 teaspoon whole cloves

1 tablespoon broken stick cinnamon

1 pound/500g sugar

1 Place the squash, onions, bananas, raisins, and vinegar in a large nonaluminum saucepan. Tie the spices in a cheesecloth bag and add to the saucepan.

2 Bring to a boil over high heat, reduce the heat, and simmer until the squash is soft and beginning to distintegrate.

3 Add the sugar, stirring to ensure it dissolves, and simmer for 30 minutes until reduced to a thick consistency.

4 Discard the bag of spices and spoon the chutney into warm sterilized jars. Seal immediately. Cool, label, and store in the refrigerator.

# Zucchini and Ginger Jam

Makes 4-6 jars

2 pounds/1kg large zucchini, peeled, seeded, and cut into small slices

4¾ cups/1kg granulated sugar

grated zest and juice of 1 large lemon

1 ounce/30g fresh ginger, a piece about 2 inches/5cm wide and ½ inch/1cm thick

1  The day before: Toss together the zucchini, sugar, lemon zest and juice into a preserving pan or large heavy-bottomed nonaluminum saucepan and let stand overnight.

2  The next day, crush the ginger with a hammer and put it in a little cheesecloth bag. Add this to the pan.

3  Stir the mixture over low heat until all the sugar has dissolved. Bring to a boil and simmer gently until the zucchini is quite translucent (about 35 minutes) and test the gel for setting on a cold saucer. (When the jelly breaks off from the spoon in a sheet or "flake," it is set.) Remove the bag of ginger before pouring the jam into hot sterilized jelly jars. Seal when hot; label when cold. Store in the refrigerator.

# Pumpkin and Apple Jam

Makes 6-8 jars

2 pounds/1kg pumpkin, peeled, seeded, and cut into small slices

9½ cups/2kg granulated sugar

1 pound/500g tart apples, peeled, cored, and sliced

juice of 2 medium oranges

juice of 2 medium lemons

1  The day before: In a large nonaluminum bowl, layer the pumpkin with 4¾ cups/1kg of the sugar.

2  In another bowl, mix the apple slices with the orange and lemon juices. Cover both bowls with cloths and let stand overnight.

3  The next day: Tip the pumpkin, together with the sugar and liquid that will have been drawn out overnight, into a large heavy nonaluminum saucepan. Add the apples and the citrus juices, and finally the rest of the sugar. Heat gently, stirring frequently, to ensure that the sugar is completely dissolved.

4  Bring to a boil and simmer gently for 30–45 minutes, until the mixture is thick, clear, and syrupy. Test for setting on a cold saucer, as above.

5  Fill hot sterilized jelly jars with the mixture, cover, and seal while hot. Label when cold. Store in the refrigerator.

# directory

There are probably in excess of 500 different cultivars of pumkins and squashes. The following directory is just a selection that I have grown myself and can recommend. They are divided into five horticultural groups (see pages 16-17): summer squash and zucchini, autumn squash, winter squash, pumpkins, and ornamentals. There are some for every situation and to suit all tastes and requirements: huge ones, little ones, orange, blue, green, and yellow ones. They come from all over the world — North America, Australia, South Africa, Great Britain, France, Italy, and Germany. A list of suppliers on pages 118–119 will help the more adventurous grower to obtain seed. The directory entries marked with an asterisk tend not to be readily available in North America, but can be obtained through the foreign sources mentioned.

# Summer Squashes & Zucchini
## (*Cucurbita pepo*)

### Arlessa Zucchini
Trailing habit. Glossy green fruit flecked with lighter green, firm flesh, and delicious flavor. Keeps well, has a thin skin so is edible even when large, and crops well into fall.

### Black Beauty
Bush habit. Well established American cultivar that has dark green fruit, flecked with pale green, and creamy white flesh. Most delicious picked when 6 to 8 in./15 to 20cm long.

### Burpee Golden Zucchini
Bush habit. Bright golden, regularly shaped fruit with dense cream-colored flesh, best picked when 4 to 6 in./10 to 15cm long.

### Clarimore Lebanese Zucchini
Bush habit. Smooth fruit is pastel green with rounded ends and a thin skin. Flesh is creamy colored and exceptionally tasty. Crops heavily in both warm and cool climates.

### Clarita (F₁) *
Bush habit. Compact, vigorous, hybrid Lebanese type, this short, club-shaped zucchini is pale green and speckled with cream-colored spots. Tender flesh.

### Condor (F₁)
Bush habit. Matures quickly yielding big crops of narrow, bright, glossy, medium dark green fruit, flecked pale green, tasty large or small. Vigorous, open plants with spineless stems and leaves, making them easy to harvest.

### Custard Yellow *
Bush habit. Pattypan type. Bright yellow, flat fruit, with scalloped edge and creamy white flesh. Good to eat young, ornamental when mature.

### Early Prolific Straightneck
Award-winning American yellow cultivar of summer squash productive throughout season. Fruit has tender, delicious flesh and can be eaten when 4 to 12 in./10 to 30cm long.

### Early White
Semi-bush habit. Flagon-shaped zucchini, pale green in color, flecked with cream. Delicious flavor, and its shape makes it perfect for stuffing.

### Early White Bush Scallop
Bush habit, pattypan type. Most frequently grown form of scallop squash. Green-white initially, maturing to wax-white. Edible when young, but most decorative when mature, resembling candles. The prominent scallops can be turned up in some fruit and down in others.

### Florentino
Semi-bush habit. This early-cropping variety should be harvested at 8 in./20cm. The fruit is ridged and striped light and dark green, and has creamy flesh.

### Gold Rush Zucchini
Bush habit. An All-American winner very similar to Burpee Golden Zucchini with uniform, narrow fruit. The color is rich yellow and the stem, a contrasting green. Smooth, thin skin and an abundance of female flowers make it good for cooking.

### Green Patty *
Bush habit. Like Peter Pan, a mini-vegetable, suitable for small gardens. Should be picked young, yielding heavy crops in 65 days and throughout summer. Best steamed.

### Greyzini (F₁)
Bush habit. Early, good cropper maturing into large, attractive, and tasty fruit. Fairly plump, ribbed fruit of medium green, speckled with yellow-green and dark green.

### Little Gem *
Trailing habit. Smaller than Rolet but similar in spread and yield. Does not keep as well as Rolet. Good baked whole.

### Milano Zucchini
Bush habit. Dark green fruit should be harvested when very young to preserve the delicate flavor and texture.

### Mongo
Bush habit. Firm, tasty, mid green zucchini with paler flecks. Best picked young, as it loses its qualities when bigger than 8 in./20cm, but yields are good.

### Onyx (F₁) *
Medium green color with yellow-cream flecks; regularly shaped fruit with small, yellow-green ridges. High yielding zucchini maturing in about 55 days.

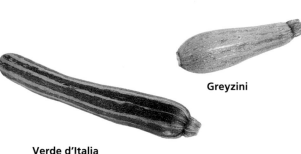
**Verde d'Italia**

**Greyzini**

**Clarita**

**Ronde de Nice**

**Mongo**

### Peter Pan (F$_1$)

Bush habit, pattypan type. Compact, light green summer squash with scalloped edges. Optimum yield when cut at 1½ in./4cm across. Best eaten young, but retains nutty flavor if left to grow a little bigger.

### Raven

Bush habit. Very early summer squash taking only about 42 days to produce fruit. Smooth, glossy, and dark green with a delicate tender flesh. Can be picked with the blossoms still attached or allowed to grow larger.

### Rolet

Trailing habit. Baseball-sized fruit, slightly larger than Little Gem, matures in late summer, high yielding. Black-green color of fruit is retained for a long time, eventually turning bronze-orange.

### Ronde de Nice

Bush habit. Old French variety of round zucchini that is pale green, flecked with creamy yellow. Very productive, can be cut from 2 to 4 in./5 to 10cm. Best steamed when small, useful shape for stuffing when larger.

### Scallop Scallopini

Bush habit, pattypan type. Early dark green summer squash shaped like a spinning top when young, flattening out as it grows. Best when picked 2 to 3 in./5 to 8cm across.

### Seneca Prolific (F$_1$)

Bush habit. One of the best tasting pale yellow straightneck summer squashes, this cultivar has a pale green stem. Early to mature and best picked at 4 to 6 in./10 to 15cm when it yields its greatest crop.

### Sunburst (F$_1$)

Bush habit, pattypan type. Prolific golden yellow, flat scalloped squash. Most tasty at 3 in./7.5cm. Decorative when grown to 5 in./12.5cm or more.

### Sundance (F$_1$)

Bush habit. Bright yellow crookneck summer squash with smooth skin. Creamy white flesh at its best when fruit is 4 to 6 in./10 to 15cm long. Can be allowed to grow for decoration.

### Superset

Bush habit. Thin-skinned, bright yellow crookneck squash with a creamy-textured flesh and delicate nutty flavor. Plants crop early and continue until late fall.

### Table Dainty

(*See* Autumn Squashes.)

### Tiger Cross (F$_1$)

(*See* Autumn Squashes.)

### Tromboncino

Trailing habit. Long thin fruits become bell-shaped at the flower end, should be harvested between 8 to 18 in./20 to 45cm long, and have firm flesh and sweet flavor. If left in the field to harden off, they can be used decoratively.

### Verde d'Italia * (Cocozelle Long Type)

Bush habit. Distinctive Italian cultivar with long, narrow regular fruit that are dark green with strongly pronounced light green stripes. It retains its narrowness as it grows, making it useful whenever it is picked.

### White Bush

Bush habit. Pale green fruit that keeps and remains tasty if left to grow to 6 or 8 in./15 to 20cm. As it reaches maturity, color fades to creamy white. High yielding cultivar.

### Yellow Summer Crookneck

(*See* Ornamentals.)

### Zahra (F$_1$)

Bush habit. Particularly early cropper, maturing in about 6 weeks. This Cousa or Middle Eastern type zucchini is characteristically chunky in shape, tapering towards the stem. Best when picked no bigger than 4 in./10cm, but is an ideal shape for stuffing if slightly larger. The plants are open and easy to pick.

### Zucchini (F$_1$)

Bush habit. Popular early variety that matures quickly. Produces a prolific number of dark green fruits that are first-class vegetables for the table. Pick from 4 to 8 in./10 to 20cm.

### Zuchlong Hybrid

Bush habit. Classic zucchini with dark green skin, finely stippled with yellow-green. An early, heavy cropper and tastes best at 6 to 8 in./15 to 20cm long.

**Burpee Golden Zucchini**

**Little Gem**

**White Bush**

**Onyx**

**Peter Pan**

# Autumn Squashes
## (*Cucurbita pepo*)

### Badger Cross (F₁) *

Bush habit. A recent hybrid, it is a prolific cropper with dark green fruit, attractively striped paler green. Has an open habit (making it easy to crop) and good cucumber mosaic virus resistance.

### Cream of the Crop (F₁)

Semi-bush habit. One of the best acorn squash, producing an abundant crop of uniform fruit weighing up to 2 lb/1 kg. Creamy white with characteristically pronounced ridges. Flesh is cream colored.

### Longue de Nice *

Trailing habit. Excellent French cultivar that has long, light, solid, rather dull green fruit reaching 2 ft./60cm in length. Prominent round bulbous shape at flower end and dense flesh.

### Orangetti *

Bush habit. Bred in Israel, one of the most attractive spaghetti squash with smaller, sweeter-tasting fruit than others. Orange, lightly mottled pale skin with orange flesh requiring less cooking time than others to obtain "spaghetti" *al dente*.

### Pasta Hybrid

Trailing habit. A very productive spaghetti squash that gives 10 to 12 in./25 to 30cm creamy yellow fruits that are low in calories and have a good texture and flavor.

### Stripetti

Trailing habit. Spaghetti squash. Hybrid showing Delica x Spaghetti parentage; green stripes on pale yellow-green background; good flavor. Stores well for 2 to 3 months.

### Swan White

Semi-bush habit. Acorn squash. Prolific, slightly yellow cream cultivar with pale yellow flesh. Fruits are about 6 in./15cm across and have a delicate, nutty flavor.

### Table Ace (F₁)

Semi-bush habit. Darkest green (nearly black) acorn squash with the typical acorn ridges with a pointed base. This is one of the first acorn-type to mature and is very productive. Fruit weighs from 1 to 2 lb./0.5 to 1kg and will store for a long time at a cool room temperature. Flesh is solid and orange, becoming a little floury when kept for too long.

### Table Dainty *

Trailing habit. Prolific variety with compact, blunt-ended fruit rarely more than 9 in./23cm long, striped dark green and yellow. Good to eat at about 4 in./10cm, but larger fruits are a useful size for stuffing. Keeps well and retains a good flavor.

### Table Queen

Semi-bush habit. Dark green acorn squash that can measure up to 8 in./20cm from stem to pointed end. Orange flesh has a distinct nutty flavor and is dry and sweet when baked.

### Tiger Cross (F₁)

Bush habit. One of earliest hybrid marrow cultivars with heavily mottled dark skin, striped creamy yellow. Good cropper with uniform straight fruit. Best picked at about 1 ft./30cm long, but can easily reach a hefty 2 ft./60cm or more.

### Tivoli (F₁)

Bush habit. Classic spaghetti squash variety that reaches 9 in./23cm and weighs up to 4 lb./2kg. Smooth, oblong-shaped fruit is yellow-cream in color with the palest green flesh (*see* page 71). Plants are very compact, only 2 ft./60cm across so it is ideal for small gardens.

### Vegetable Marrow

Bush habit. The white fruit is best harvested at 6 to 8 in./15 to 20 cm and has a slightly nutty flavor.

### Vegetable Spaghetti

Trailing habit. The light yellow fruits have a somewhat oblong shape and should be picked when about 8 in./20cm long. Store in a cool, dry place.

**Tiger Cross**

**Table Dainty**

**Orangetti**

**Table Ace**

**Cream of the Crop**

# Winter Squashes
## (*Cucurbita maxima*)

except where stated otherwise

### Amber Cup

Trailing habit. Kabocha type. The small fruits average 3 to 5 lb./1.4 to 2.2kg and have a sweet, dry flesh that is delicious baked and contains less starch than most varieties. Distinctive scarlet skin makes it easy to find the fruit under the foliage.

### Black Forest

Trailing habit. Sometimes called Buttonless Buttercup. This squash is similar to Sweet Mama, being typical of Kabocha type, but smaller. Same flattened shape, dark green, striped gray-green skin and fairly dry, sweet, deep orange flesh. Matures early and keeps well. Ideal size for baking and stuffing.

### Bleu de Hongrie *

Trailing habit. Old Central European cultivar that is a flattened globe about 10 in./25cm wide and 6 in./15cm high, weighing up to 10 lb./5kg. Fine, china-like pale gray-blue skin is easy to peel, and firm orange flesh is ideal for making soups.

### Blue Ballet

Trailing habit. Smooth- skinned, medium-sized hubbard squash usually weighing 4 lb./2kg, with pronounced point at stalk end and rounded at flower end. Metallic blue with bright orange, smooth-textured flesh. Quick maturing and stores well.

### Buttercup

Trailing habit. Small, dumpy, dark green squash, with gray-green stripes, and gray-green button at flower end. Fruits weigh between 3 to 5 lb./1.5 to 2.5kg and have deep orange, fiberless flesh, which has an intense, rich, sweet flavor.

### Butternut
### (*Cucurbita moschata*)

Trailing habit. Group of some of the most appreciated winter squash. Nutty, rich orange flesh is sweetest when fully mature after about three months of storage and keeps for up to a year. Pear-shaped fruit is distinctive buff color. Among best cultivars to look out for are Ponca (smooth and cylindrical, weighing 2 to 3 lb./1 to 1.5kg and probably earliest maturing open-pollinating butternut); Waltham (more widely pear-shaped and larger, weighing 4 to 5 lb./2.5kg) and some $F_1$ hybrids such as Sprinter, Ultra, and Nicklow's Delight.

### Chestnut

Semi-bush habit. Small, flat-based squash that weighs 3 to 4 lb./1.5 to 2kg. Gray-green, barely ridged skin and modest rise at stalk end. The flesh is fiberless with dry texture, its sweetness increasing in the weeks after harvesting.

### Citrouille d'Eysines à Potage *

Trailing habit. Old French cultivar, this most striking pale, creamy orange squash has corky growths in varying quantities all over the skin. Fruit can be large, weighing up to 20 lb./10kg, and the orange, slightly grainy flesh is best used for soups.

### Crown Prince ($F_1$) *

Trailing habit. New Zealand cultivar frequently seen in Britain. Shape of a slightly flattened globe, measuring approx. 12 in./30cm across, with slight ridges all around and sometimes a tiny button at flower end. Metallic blue skin. Deep orange flesh is delicious baked, roasted, boiled, or steamed. Will keep for up to 6 months.

### Delicata
### (*Cucurbita pepo*)

Semi-trailing habit. Sweet potato type. Cylindrical creamy white squash with dark green stripes and flecks,

**Citrouille d'Eysines à Potage**

**Queensland Blue**

**Flat White Boer**

**Crown Prince**

7 to 9 in./17.5 to 23cm long and 3 in./7.5cm wide, weighing 1½ to 2 lb./0.75 to 1kg. Sweet yellow flesh and large seed cavity, making it ideal for stuffing. Good immediately after harvest, but stores well.

### Ebony Acorn
### (Cucurbita pepo)

Trailing habit. Developed at Cornell University in the mid-1950s, it has become the standard squash for baking in the U.S. It is best eaten within four months of harvesting, but it doesn't need sun curing or the very dry storage of most winter squash. Fruit average 2 lb./1kg and have very dark green, ribbed skin. The slightly nutty to sweet flesh is a pale orange-buff color and has a dry flaky texture.

### Emerald Bush Buttercup

Bush habit. Ideal for small gardens. Deep orange, sweet-potato-type flesh is moist, sweet, and fiberless. The long-keeping fruits are chunky with

flattened ridges and a small blossom cup. Skin is gray-green in color. They average 3 to 4 lb./1.4 to 1.8kg.

### Flat White Boer *

Trailing habit. South African cultivar, flattest, slightly ridged, white fruit. Dark, dense orange flesh has fine flavor. Ideal for all forms of cooking. Needs long growing season, but good keeper.

### Futsu Black *
### (Cucurbita moschata)

Trailing habit. This squash of Japanese origin doesn't resemble in any way other members of the group, but has the characteristic star-shaped stem base. Round, slightly ridged fruit has a diameter of 4 to 6 in./10 to 15cm and is dark green when young. Matures to an orange-brown with beautiful bloom. Weighs between 1 and 3 lb./0.5 and 1.5kg and has deep yellow-orange flesh, which is firm, sweet, and nutty.

### Gold Nugget

Bush habit. Prolific, early maturing small squash, weighing at most 2 lb./1kg. Deep apricot-orange, smooth skin and orange flesh with a flavor similar to Buttercup. Ideal for baking.

### Golden Delicious

Trailing habit. Variant of Golden Hubbard, but slightly blunter in shape at stalk end, making it more heart-shaped. Thick orange skin is smooth and deep orange, fiberless flesh is sweet.

### Golden Hubbard

Trailing habit. Most common hubbard cultivar, can weigh up to 15 lb./7.5kg, but usually less. Characteristic shape with pronounced points at both ends. Skin is golden yellow to orange and more or less warty. Orange flesh is sweet and dry textured and ideal for cooking and baking, especially for pies. Good keeper. Can be used for decorative purposes if hardened.

### Green Delicious

Trailing habit. Medium-sized fruit weighs in at about 4 lb./1.8kg, is dark green, and keeps well. The orange flesh is smooth, flavorful, and high in vitamins.

### Green Hubbard

Trailing habit. Cultivated since 1790. This is, perhaps, the most intensely flavored hubbard. Large fruit usually weighs about 10 to 12 lb./5 to 6kg. Dark green skin is more or less warty, and fruit has prominent points at both ends. Vigorous grower and another good keeper. There is also a miniature form of this variety with fruits that average 2 lb./1kg.

### Honey Delight

Trailing habit. A Kabocha type squash with flattened fruits that are dark green with lighter stripes and weigh 4 to 6 lb./1.8 to 2.7kg. Flesh is bright orange with a sweet, dry, flaky texture when cooked. Stores well.

**Green Hubbard**

**Bleu de Hongrie**

**Sweet Mama**

**Golden Hubbard**

### Melonette Jaspée de Vendée *
### (*Cucurbita pepo*)

Trailing habit. Old French cultivar from the Atlantic Coast area. Looks like small, smooth melon with beautiful golden yellow color. Orange flesh is sweet and delicious – good for pies and puddings. Keeps until the spring.

### Mooregold

Trailing habit. Cultivar developed at the University of Wisconsin. Early maturing small squash weighing up to 2½ lb./1.25kg. Orange skin mottled and lightly striped apricot; flower end attractively stained black. Nutty flesh is particularly good steamed and as a purée.

### New England Blue Hubbard

Trailing habit. Most striking of hubbards, this cultivar has metallic blue, predominantly warty skin and good shape with points at both ends. Weighs up to 25 lb./12.5kg, but usually between 12 to 20 lb./6 to 10kg. Yellow flesh is slightly moist and not too sweet.

### Pink Jumbo Banana

Trailing habit. As name suggests, a huge, banana-shaped squash, weighing up to 50 lb./25kg. Attractive peachy pink color with good quality slightly grainy flesh. Traditionally used as cattle fodder.

### Queensland Blue *

Trailing habit. Favorite Australian cultivar of dark gray-green color, and prominently ribbed. Fruit usually two tiered, resembling an old-fashioned gelatin mold. Up to 10 in./25cm across and 10 lb./5kg in weight. Brown-orange flesh is nutty and smooth textured.

### Red Kuri (Uchiki Kuri)

Trailing habit. Onion-shaped, bright orange-red squash weighing 4 to 8 lb./2 to 4kg. Dense textured, nutty, orange flesh and a particularly high content of vitamins and trace elements.

### Sugar Loaf
### (*Cucurbita pepo*)

Trailing habit. Sweet potato type. New cultivar, developed at Oregon State University, intermediate between Delicata and Sweet Dumpling varieties. Up to 6 in./15cm long and 4 in./10cm wide with sweet flavor. Flesh is slightly floury. Good for cooking straight after harvest, but can also be stored successfully.

### Sweet Dumpling

(*See* Ornamentals.)

### Sweet Mama

Trailing habit. Typical Kabocha squash with flattened-globe shape and dark green, practically black skin with faint gray-green stripes. Usually weighs about 4 to 5 lb./2 to 2.5kg. Delicious flesh is dark yellow and dry in texture. Very good keeper.

### Sweet Meat

Trailing habit. Fast maturing and good keeping winter squash with delicious deep orange, firm, sweet flesh. Fruit have a tough greeny blue skin and weigh between 6 to 15 lb./3 to 7.5kg. This variety produces well on dry sites, and can be frozen without turning mealy.

### Winter Luxury
### (*Cucurbita pepo*)

Trailing habit. A variety introduced in 1893. Looks like a large cantaloupe. Fine netting over orange skin. Fruit reaches 9 in./23cm, weighing up to 8 lb./4kg. Sweet, dark orange flesh and keeps successfully for several months.

### Zipinki Campana

(*See* Ornamentals.)

**Butternut**

**Winter Luxury**

**Melonette Jaspée de Vendée**

**Futsu Black**

# Pumpkins
## *(Cucurbita pepo)*
except where stated otherwise

### Appalachian (F$_1$)
Semi-bush habit. Similar to Howden but with uniform fruit that matures at 25 to 30 lb./11 to 13kg.

### Aspen (F$_1$)
Semi-bush habit. Tall, globe-shaped pumpkin is green when young, maturing early to dark orange. Uniform fruit reach up to 30 lb./15kg.

### Atlantic Giant
### *(Cucurbita maxima)*
Trailing habit. This variety has produced world champions recently breaking 1,000 lb./450kg barrier. Plants grown from commercial seed (look for selections including the name Dill in them) easily reach 70 to 100 lb./35 to 50kg. Most fruit is yellow throughout growing season.

### Autumn Gold
Trailing habit. Medium-sized, tall, globe-shaped fruit, gold when young, maturing to orange, and weighing around 10 lb./5kg.

### Baby Bear
Trailing habit. High yielding small cultivar. Fruit weigh 1½ to 2 lb./0.75 to 1kg. Green when young, ripening to orange. Flesh good to eat; semi-naked seed can be roasted for snacks. Decorative alongside other ornamentals.

### Baby Boo
(*See* Ornamentals.)

### Big Max
### *(Cucurbita maxima)*
Trailing habit. Another monster that is an attractive peach to pale apricot color which can reach 100 lb./50kg.

### Big Moon
Trailing habit. Giant pumpkin weighing up to 200 lb./90kg, but flesh is good for pies. Needs a long growing season.

### Caspar
Trailing habit. A quick maturing variety with a pure white skin and orange flesh that looks most unusual when carved. The fruits are round with flattened ends and average 10 lb./5kg in weight.

### Cinderella
Bush habit. Similar to, but smaller than Rouge Vif d'Etampes. Flattish, slightly ridged fruit of deep orange color with black mark around flower end. Weighs between 10 and 15 lb./5 to 7.5kg.

### Connecticut Field
Trailing habit. Old Halloween pumpkin with good, tall globe shape, green, turning to deep orange. Moderately productive, and fruits weigh from 12 to 20 lb./6 to 10kg.

### Frosty (F$_1$)
Semi-bush habit. The bright orange, oval-shaped pumpkins average 15 to 20 lb./7 to 9kg and have a very uniform color. Early maturing, can be used for pies or carving.

### Funny Face
Bush habit. An early variety that can be used for pies or decoration. The slightly ribbed fruits are 12 to 15 lb./6 to 7kg and have golden yellow flesh with a small seed cavity.

### Ghostrider
Trailing habit. Another classic Halloween pumpkin with robust handle and very similar to Connecticut Field in shape, color, and weight. It is, however, perhaps the most widely grown open-pollinated variety.

### Howden
Trailing habit. Selection of Connecticut Field, this tall, globe-shaped fruit is ridged and green when immature, turning dark orange. Usually weighs between 15 and 25 lb./7.5 and 12.5kg, but can reach over 30 lb./15kg.

### Jack-be-Little
Trailing habit. Tiny version of Rouge Vif d'Etampes measuring 4 in./10cm across and just over 2 in./5cm high with deep ridges. Good orange color with fine flesh making it good to bake. Also highly decorative.

### Jack of All Trades
Semi-bush habit. The almost ball-shaped fruits have a good handle and are bright orange with shallow ribs. They weigh in at 15 to 20 lb./7 to 9kg.

**Aspen**

**Rouge Vif d'Etampes**

**Tom Fox**

## Jack O' Lantern

Trailing habit. Ideal Halloween lantern. Variable cultivar — oval and round fruit, 12 to 16 in./30 to 40cm across and weighing from 8 to 14 lb./4 to 7kg. Good, tough, orange skin (green when immature), making it suitable to carve.

## Jackpot (F₁)

Trailing habit. Consistently good, round pumpkin measuring 10 in./25cm across and weighing 10 to 14 lb./5 to 7kg. Green when young, turning bright orange, with good-quality pie flesh.

## Little Lantern

Trailing habit. Similar to Baby Bear and Spooktacular. Miniature variety with smooth fruits 5 in./12cm across, slightly ribbed, and bright orange.

## Lumina

Trailing type. Wonderful pumpkin. Pure creamy white with intense orange flesh. It is 8 to 10 in./20 to 25cm across, weighing up to 12 lb./6kg. Useful for carving and decorative use (*see* page 34).

## Mammoth
### (*Cucurbita maxima*)

Trailing habit. Most important group of giant pumpkins ranging from yellow to orange. Can reach 100 lb./45kg, but usually less. Skin can become slightly cracked or appear netted when ripe.

## Munchkin

(*See* Ornamentals.)

## New England Pie (Small Sugar)

Trailing habit. Fruit are green when young, becoming orange with maturity. Globe-shaped and not too big, weighing 5 to 8 lb./2.5 to 4kg. Starchy, dry, flesh is ideal for processing and baking.

## Prizewinner Hybrid
### (*Cucurbita maxima*)

Trailing habit. Giant pumpkin that will grow to over 300 lb./150kg. Fruit is globe-shaped with shiny, smooth, deep yellow to orange color.

## Rocket (F₁)

Trailing habit. Good for carving, green when young, ripening to orange. Heavy for size (12 to 20 lb./6 to 10kg). Quick to mature, has some ribbing and strong green handle; great resistance to rot.

## Rouge Vif d'Etampes
### (*Cucurbita maxima*)

Trailing habit. One of best large French varieties. Bright red-orange, flat, deeply ridged fruit, up to 2 ft./60cm in diameter, weighing up to 25 lb./12.5kg. Flesh is good for soups and puddings.

## Small Sugar

(*See* New England Pie.)

## Spirit (F₁)

Trailing habit. Another Halloween pumpkin with regular round fruit about 10 in./25cm in diameter and weighing 10 to 14 lb./5 to 7kg. Can be grown in restricted spaces.

## Spooktacular (F₁)

Trailing habit. Small pie pumpkin. High yield of regular, slightly flattened globe-shaped orange fruit, 6 in./15cm across, which weigh 2 to 4 lb./1 to 2kg. Vigorous, early ripening with tasty flesh.

## Sumo (F₁) *
### (*Cucurbita maxima*)

Trailing habit. Huge round pumpkin with beautiful orange color. Irregular ridges give impression of Sumo wrestler. Reaches 200 lb./100kg, but 50 lb./25kg makes a good-sized fruit.

## Sunny *

Trailing habit. The magical yellow gene ensures that this hybrid cultivar colors early in the season, and its speed of growth makes it ideal for short growing seasons. About 10 in./25cm across and weighing 6 to 8 lb./3 to 4kg. Sweet flesh delicious in soups and pies.

## Sweetie Pie

(*See* Ornamentals.)

## Tom Fox (F₁)

Trailing habit. Halloween pumpkin that bears name of New Hampshire dairy farmer who developed it. Robust, ridged, dark orange fruits (green when immature) vary slightly in shape and size, with strong, nearly black handles. Weighs in at 6 to 12 lb./3 to 6kg, heavy for its size, and stores well.

## Trick or Treat

Trailing habit. A double purpose pumpkin with 6 lb./3kg fruits that make good lanterns and have hulless seeds good for toasting and eating.

## Triple Treat

Trailing habit. Late pie pumpkin a little difficult to germinate, due to its naked seeds. Deep orange fruit (green when young), about same size as that of New England Pie and weigh up to 8 lb./4kg. Sweet flesh and good for keeping.

Jack O'Lantern

Sunny

Jackpot

Spooktacular

Jack-be-Little

# Ornamentals

### Aladdin's Turban
### (Cucurbita maxima)

Trailing habit, turban type. Good form with smaller fruit than Turk's Turban, (to 8 in./20cm). Distinctive, slightly dull orange and green stripes appearing to have been painted on with a brush. Medium vigor.

### d'Albenga *
### (Cucurbita moschata)

Trailing habit. Looks rather like a butternut gone wrong. Long, crooked neck with a bulbous end and pale beige skin when ripe. The flesh is characteristic of *C. moschata*, dense, deep orange, and juicy.

### Baby Boo
### (Cucurbita pepo)

Trailing habit, mini-pumpkin type. Miniature, creamy white fruit about 3 in./7.5cm across and 2 in./5cm high, with deep ridges. Decorative and has fine creamy flesh. Not too vigorous.

### BOTTLE GOURDS
### (Lagenaria siceraria)

Birdhouse gourd — Also known as the pilgrim's bottle gourd. Bilobed with rounded base and smaller upper chamber, from 8 to 10 in./20 to 25cm high.

Canteen — Broad pear-shaped gourd that can be quart- to gallon-sized. Shoulder strap of agave fiber or hemp is knotted around bulb to make a sling for carrying. Base is often cut to make large bowl. Tarahumara Canteen and Tepehuan Canteen are typical examples.

Dipper — Round bulbous base is topped with a straight-sided handle of varying length from 8 to 18 in./20 to 45cm. Base is opened on side to serve as a scoop.

Flat Corsican — Completely flat gourd approximately 8 in./20cm across, used in Roman times as a hip flask.

Peyote Ceremonial — Smallest bottle gourd, 4 in./10cm high – it was used for smoking hallucinogenic Mexican cactus and as a container for curare.

Snake (Cucuzzi) — Long, almost cylindrical gourd, sometimes reaching 3 ft./1m. If grown on the ground, it curls into a serpentine shape, but when climbing, hangs down straight.

T & M Large Bottle — Flat-based bottle shape with a long, tapered neck, approximately 15 in./37.5cm in height.

### Cave Man's Club

Trailing habit. The knobby fruit have a long neck and resemble a long-handled club.

### Crown of Thorns
### (Cucurbita pepo)

Trailing habit, ornamental gourd. Striking cultivar with tentacular growths around fruit. Most commonly white with green stripes, but also green, yellow, green and yellow, and with green and yellow stripes.

### Custard Yellow

(*See* Summer Squashes & Zucchini.)

### Dolphin

Trailing habit. Dark green fruit that are ridged like a turtle shell and have a long neck.

### Early White Bush Scallop

(*See* Summer Squashes & Zucchini.)

### Fig-leaf gourd *
### (Cucurbita ficifolia)

Trailing habit. Extremely vigorous species, native of Mexico, also known as Malabar gourd or Sidra. Stems can reach from 30 to 35 ft./10 to 12m, with leaves reminiscent of those of the fig. Fruit are bluntly egg-shaped, between 6 and 14 in./15 and 35cm long, and attractively mottled green and cream. White edible flesh is rather bland and breaks up into strands when cooked.

### Gold Nugget

(*See* Winter Squashes.)

### Jack-be-Little

(*See* Pumpkins.)

### Mini Red Turban
### (Cucurbita maxima)

Smallest and least elegant turban gourd, usually about 4 in./10cm across and sometimes larger. Bright orange to red turban, edged in green, tops a white, slightly warty button. The plant is not overwhelmingly vigorous and is moderately prolific.

**Bottle gourd**

**Fig-leaf gourd**

**Turk's Turban**

**d'Albenga**

**Zipinki Campana**

## Munchkin
### (Cucurbita pepo)

Trailing habit, mini-pumpkin type. Nearly identical to both Jack-be-Little and Sweetie Pie. Tiny, ridged pumpkin, prolific, useful in table decorations or for serving individual portions of soup or mousse.

## ORNAMENTAL GOURDS
### (Cucurbita pepo)

Apple gourd — Trailing habit. Spherical fruit with smooth white skin. Prolific but not too vigorous.

Miniature ball gourd — Trailing habit. Small round fruit, about 2½ in./5cm across. White, yellow, or with dark green background and paler speckles.

Nest egg/White egg gourd — Trailing habit. Very vigorous plants, fruit same size as hen's egg and white in color.

Orange ball gourd — Trailing habit. Resembles an orange, both in size and color; one of most striking gourds.

Pear bicolor gourd — Trailing habit. One of the most common forms. Elongated shape with roundish swelling at flower end. Colors range from white to dark green. Patterns include pale green longitudinal stripes on dark green, or lemon-yellow on bright canary; bicolored stripes of half yellow, half green; and green stripes circling the fruit. Different combinations can appear together with, for example, solid yellow neck and striped green base.

Mayo warty bute/Orange warted gourd — Fruit mostly round from 2 to 4 in./5 to 10cm, but sometimes pear-shaped with bubbles on the surface. Usually orange or white, but sometimes green.

Small spoon — Oval-based fruit with a long slender "handle" about 6 to 8 in./15 to 20cm long.

White-striped flat gourd — Trailing habit. Vigorous strain, distinctive by both shape and color. Approximately 3 in./7.5cm across, but only 1½ to 2 in./3 to 5cm high, with stripes against a mottled green and cream background. Stems can reach up to 14 ft./2.8m, and leaves are distinctly five-lobed with sharply pointed tips. Grows well on a trellis.

## Peter Pan

(*See* Summer Squashes & Zucchini.)

## Speckled Swan

Trailing habit. This can give either small or large fruits that are dark green speckled with cream and have a swan-like neck and head. For large fruit, up to 18 in./45cm long, allow one fruit per plant.

## Sunburst

(*See* Summer Squashes & Zucchini.)

## Sweet Dumpling
### (Cucurbita pepo)

Trailing habit. A favorite for decorative and culinary use, making one-portion cups that are pale cream with dark green stripes. Round in shape and 4 in./10cm across with firm, tender orange flesh. Can be stored for 3 to 4 months.

## Sweetie Pie
### (Cucurbita pepo)

Trailing habit, mini-pumpkin type. Similar in shape and color to Jack-be-Little and Munchkin with deep orange ridges. Smallest of the three, reaching no more than 3 in./7.5cm across by 2 in./5cm high.

## Tristar *
### (Cucurbita maxima)

Trailing habit. Oddly shaped blue-green winter squash with three bulbous lobes that curl into the stem. Good light yellow flesh. Keeps well.

## Turk's Turban
### (Cucurbita maxima)

Trailing habit, turban type. Most commonly found turban squash, this cultivar has large fruit up to 10 in./25 cm across. Turban is dark orange and button irregularly striped orange, green, and cream. Edible flesh.

## Yellow Summer Crookneck

Bush habit. Old American yellow warty summer squash variety in cultivation since mid-19th century. Firm, tender, pale green flesh that has its best flavor when cut from 4 to 6 in./10 to 15cm.

## Zipinki Campana *

Bush habit. Small, quick maturing squash, originally from Argentina. Somewhat like Gold Nugget but bronze-green, mottled cream, and rust, with very hard skin. Onion-shaped with shallow ridges. Flesh is orange and firm.

**Sweet Dumpling**

**Mayo warty bute**

**Orange warted gourd**

**Crookneck**

**Striped pear gourd**

**Bi colored pear gourd**

**Sweetie Pie**

# Suppliers

## Australia

**Attunga Home Garden Seed and Bulbs**
57 Radford Road,
Reservoir,
Victoria 3073
Tel: 613 97 937500

**Mr Fothergill's Seeds Pty Ltd**
8 Annagrove Road,
Rouse Hill,
Sydney 2153,
New South Wales
Tel: 612 98 380500

## Canada

**Dominion Seed House**
Box 2500
Georgetown,
ON L7G 5L6
Tel: 905 873 3037

**Howard Dill**
R.R.1 Windsor
Nova Scotia B0N 2T0
Tel: 902 798 2728

**Stokes Seeds Ltd.**
39 James Street, Box 10
St. Catherines,
ON L2R 6R6
Tel: 905 688 4300

## France

**Graines Baumaux**
B.P. 100,
54062 Nancy Cedex
Tel: 383 15 86 86

## Germany

**Carl Sperling & Co**
P.O. Box 2640
21316 Luneburg
Tel: 4131 30170

## Italy

**Fratelli Ingegnoli-Milano**
Corso Beunos Aires 54
Milano
Tel: 2295 20521

## South Africa

**Starke Ayres**
Box/Bus 304,
Eppindust 7475
Cape Town/Kaapstad
Tel: 21 543231

## United Kingdom

**S E Marshalls & Co Ltd**
Wisbech,
Cambridge
PE13 2RF
Tel: 01945 583407

**Mr Fothergill's Seeds Ltd**
Kentford,
Newmarket
Suffolk
CB8 7QB
Tel: 01638 751161

**Thompson & Morgan**
London Road,
Ipswich,
Suffolk IP2 0BA
Tel: 01473 688821

## USA

**W Atlee Burpee and Co**
300 Park Avenue,
Warminster,
PA 18974
Tel: 215 674 4915

**The Cook's Garden**
P.O. Box 535,
Londonderry
VT 05148
Tel: 800 457 9703

**Ferry-Morse Seed Co**
P.O. Box 488,
Fulton, Ky 42041
Tel: 502 472 3400

**Johnny's Selected Seeds**
Foss Hill Road,
Albion,
Maine 04910
Tel: 207 437 4301

**Lake Valley Seed**
5741 Arapahoe,
Boulder, Co 80303
Tel: 303 449 4882

**The Meyer Seed Co**
Baltimore,
Maryland
Tel: 410 342 4224

**Native Seeds/ SEARCH**
2509 N Campbell Avenue 325,
Tucson, AZ 85719
Tel: 520 327 9123

**Old Sturbridge Village Seed Store**
1 Sturbridge Village Road,
Sturbridge,
Mass 01566
Tel: 508 347 3362

**Shepherd's Garden Seeds**
30 Irene Street,
Torrington
CT 06790-6658
Tel: 860 482 3638

## Mail Order

### Floral supplies

**Fox Farms**
06-684 County Road 1
Edon, OH 43518
Tel: 419 272 2278
For fresh sage leaves,
everlasting flowers, herbs,
ornamental grains, and
grasses.

**Oak Ridge Farms, Inc.**
P.O. Box 28,
Dept RD
Basking Ridge,
NJ 07920-0028
For freshly dried bay leaves
and short stemmed bunches
of sage, dried flowers and
fruits, pods, pine cones,
nuts, mosses, and essential oils.
Send $2.00 for catalogue.

**San Francisco Herb Company**
250 14th Street, Dept. RD
San Francisco
CA 94103
Tel: 800 227 4530
For high quality herbs, spices,
potpourri supplies, and
fragrance oils.

**Season's Scents**
1550 Upper James Street,
Unit 9
Hamilton,
ON L9B 2R8
For dried bay leaves, essential
oil, plus a full line of preserved
and dried flowers and greenery,
floral supplies, glycerine, silica,
fragrance, and essential oils.
Send $2.00 for complete price
list or $5.00 for color catalogue
(includes price list).

## Flours and Baking Equipment

**King Arthur® Flour Baker's Catalogue**
P.O. Box 876, Norwich
VT 05055-0876
Tel: 800 827 6836

# Societies

## Australia
**Australian Giant Pumpkin and Vegetable Society Inc**
PO Box 7032,
Karingal Centre
Victoria 3199
Tel: 613 9786 0337

## United Kingdom
**British National Pumpkin Society**
PO Box 524, Meriden,
Coventry CV7 7ZU
Tel: 01676 523339

## USA
**The American Gourd Society**
PO Box 274,
Mt Gilead,
Ohio 43338
Tel: 419 362 6446

**The Great Pumpkin Commonwealth**
445 Middlesex Avenue,
Wilmington,
Mass 01887
Tel: 508 658 5852

**The International Pumpkin Association Inc**
2155 Union Street,
San Francisco, California 94123
Tel: 415 346 4447

**World Pumpkin Confederation**
14050 Route 62
Collins, New York 14034
Tel: 716 532 5995

# Growers

*Growers open to the public in the autumn and sell pumpkins and squash:*

## Canada
**Howard Dill**
R.R.1 Windsor
Nova Scotia
BON 2T0
Tel: 902 798 2728

## France
**Le Potager Extraordinaire**
'Les Mares',
85150 La Mothe-Achard
Tel: 251 46 67 83

**Thierry Roland**
6 rue de Meaux,
60810 Barbery
Tel: 1 44 54 41 68

## United Kingdom
**C R Upton**
The Lodge,
4 Top Road,
Slindon, Arundel,
West Sussex
BN18 0RP
Tel: 01243 814219

**Plants of Special Interest Nursery**
High Street,
Braithwell,
Yorkshire S66 7AL
Tel: 01709 812328

# Festivals

*Festivals take place during September and early October. These are a selection of the most popular festivals, but it is worth looking out for others while travelling around.*

## Belgium
**Tourinnes-St-Lambert, Belgium**
For further information write to:
4 Pachis du Capitaine, 1457
Tourinnes-St-Lambert

## France
**Tranzault, Indre-et-Loire, France**
Contact Office du Tourisme de la
Chatre Tel: 254 48 22 64

**Luneville, Lorraine, France**
Contact: Mme Darembert,
Château de Gerbeviller 54830
Tel: 383 42 71 57

# Index

Illustrations are denoted by page numbers in italic

**PICTURE CREDITS**
**Marie O'Hara/Garden Picture Library** Front jacket **Jeremy Hopley** Back jacket top left and right and Spine **Steve Baxter** Back jacket bottom **John Carter** Author photo. **Bridgeman Art Library** /Private Collection/*George Adamson* 11 **Professor Stefan Buczacki** 25 bottom, 25 top **Cephas Picture Library** /TOP/*Daniel Czap* 6, 14 /15, /*Mick Rock* 29 **Corbis** /*Dave Bartruff* 48 bottom **Howard Dill Enterprises** 26 left, /*Eileen Healey* 27 top **Mary Evans Picture Library** 10 **Garden Picture Library** /*Andrea Jones* 8, /*Mayer/Le Scanff* 18, 20, /*Marianne Majerus* 23, /*Marie O'Hara* 22, /*Steven Wooster* 12 **Garden Answers** 4, 109 bottom right, 110 center right **Robert Harding Picture Library** /*Robert Cundy* 9 **Reed International Books Ltd.** /*Steve Baxter* 50, 53, 59, 63, 71, 77, 81, 85, 89, 93, 97, 101, /*Jeremy Hopley* 32, 34, 36, 38, 40, 42, 44, 46, 104, /*Jess Koppel* 107 left, 107 center right, /*James Merrell* 30, /*Tim Ridley* 16, 17, 106, 107 center, 107 right, 107 center left, 108, 109 center left, 109 center right, 109 left, 110 right, 110 left, 110 center left, 111, 112, 113, 114, 115 **Kirk Mombert** 26 right **Photo Researchers, Inc** /*Gary Retherford* 49 **South American Pictures** /*Tony Morrison* 47 **1996 World Pumpkin Confederation** 27 bottom

**AUTHOR'S ACKNOWLEDGMENTS**
Throughout the years of growing and tasting pumpkins and squash, many people have helped me and contributed to my knowledge and to the fulfilment of this book. I am particularly grateful to my husband, John Carter, who has probably done more than his fair share of pumpkin hauling and squash tasting; and to Jane Aspden who has supported the idea of a book since I first discussed it with her. Other members of the editorial staff at Mitchell Beazley, including Lucy Bridgers, Fiona Knowles and Sue Jamieson have given me support and brought all the different aspects of the book together.

I would also like to thank the following who have contributed in many different ways: Chantal Aubry, Siobhan Avis, Claude and Bernard Boisset, Jean-Marc and Penny Boisset, Nicholas and Stephanie Boisset, Camille Bultelle, Dominique Bultelle, Claudette Caven, Peter Dunstan, Brent Elliott and the staff at the RHS Lindley Library, Daria Fiozzi, Anna-Maria Fiozzi, Jean-Claude Garnaud, Jim Gardiner and staff at the RHS Garden, Wisley, particularly Jim England, Arthur Jackson, Julie Harrod, Joanna Langhorne, Kedrun Laurie, Sue Lowe, Diana Lucas, Lukman Miah, Elspeth Napier, Sandra Poynton, Michel Rialland, Pippa Sargeant, Veronica Sekules, Sabrina Shaw, Jessica and Jack Shields, Elizabeth Sisley, Conroy and Jill Smith, Mary Smith, Clare Sobieraj, Rosa Tidy, Mike Turner, Ushi Wartenberg, Jenny Watkins, Stephen Winterbottom, Melinda Wolcott, Margaret Wood.